BRITISH CAMPAIGN MEDALS

BRITISH CAMPAIGN MEDALS

Waterloo to the Gulf

Robert W. Gould
M.B.E.

ARMS AND
ARMOUR

Arms and Armour Press
A Cassell Imprint
Villiers House, 41-47 Strand, London WC2N 5JE.

Distributed in the USA by Sterling Publishing Co. Inc., 387 Park Avenue South, New York, NY 10016-8810.

Distributed in Australia by Capricorn Link (Australia) Pty. Ltd, 2/13 Carrington Road, Castle Hill, NSW 2154.

First edition 1972; second edition with price guide supplement, 1982; third edition fully revised, 1984; this edition revised with new price guide and expanded introductory text and illustrations. 1994.

British Library Cataloguing-in-Publication Data:
a catalogue record for this book is available from the British Library

ISBN 1-85409-224-3

Designed and edited by DAG Publications Ltd
Designed by David Gibbons
Printed and bound in Great Britain by
Biddles Ltd, Guildford and King's Lynn

Acknowledgements
The majority of the medals in this book were loaned by Donald Hall, and the remainder by Ronald Barden of A. H. Baldwin & Sons Ltd., and J. B. Hayward of J. B. Hayward & Son. Photography by D. J. Teague. My grateful thanks to all four for their co-operation, advice and, in the case of the photographer, patience.

CONTENTS

Introduction.....7
Where to buy Medals.....8
Classification and Condition.....9
Display and Cleaning.....9
The Collecting Field.....10
Research.....10
Eligibility of Actions.....11
The Man Behind the Medal.....11
Odd Man Out.....12
Casualties.....13
Miniatures.....16
Medal Related Collectables.....16
Figures 1 to 11.....17

Directory.....24
Where to Meet Other Collectors.....24
Where to See British Campaign Medals.....24
Auctioneers.....28
Medal Dealers.....28
Publications.....29
Bibliography.....29

Price Guide.....30

The Plates.....36
1. Waterloo Medal, 1815.....36
2. Military General Service Medal, 1793–1814.....37
3. Naval General Service Medal, 1793–1840.....38
4. Army of India Medal, 1799–1826.....41
5. Ghuznee Medal, 1839.....42
6. Candahar, Ghuznee and Cabul Medals, 1841–1842.....43
7. Jellalabad Medals, 1841–1842.....44
8. Defence of Kelat-I-Ghilzie, 1842.....44
9. First China War, 1842.....45
10. Scinde Campaign Medals, 1842.....46
11. Gwalior Campaign Stars, 1843.....46
12. Sutlej Medal, 1845–1846.....47
13. South African Campaigns, 1834–1853.....48
14. Punjab Medal, 1848–1849.....48
15. India General Service Medal, 1854–1895.....49
16. Crimean War Medal, 1854–1856.....50
17. Baltic Medal, 1854–1855.....51
18. Indian Mutiny Medal, 1857–1858.....52
19. Second China War Medal, 1857–1860.....53
20. New Zealand Medal, 1845–1847 and 1860–1866.....54
21. Canada General Service Medal, 1866–1870.....55
22. Abyssinian War Medal, 1867–1868.....56
23. Ashantee War Medal, 1873–1874.....57
24. Zulu and Basuto War Medal, 1877–1879.....58
25. Afghanistan Medal, 1878–1880.....59
26. Kabul to Kandahar Star, 1880.....60
27. Cape of Good Hope General

Service Medal, 1880–1897 60
28. Egypt Medal, 1882–1889.........60
The Khedive's Stars.................61
29. North West Canada Medal, 1885..62
30. East and West Africa, 1887 1900................................63
31. British South Africa Company's Medal, 1890–1897 64
32. Central Africa, 1891–1898.......64
33. Indian General Service Medal, 1895–1902................................65
34. Ashanti Star, 1896....................66
35. Queen's Sudan Medal, 1896–1897................................67
36. Khedive's Sudan Medal, 1896–1908................................67
37. East and Central Africa, 1897–1899................................68
38. Queen's South Africa Medal, 1899–1902................................69
39. King's South Africa Medal, 1901–1902................................70
40. Queen's Mediterranean Medal, 1899–1902 70
41. Transport Medal, 1899–1902...71
42. Third China War Medal, 1900.71
43. Ashanti Medal, 1900................72
44. Africa General Service Medal, 1902–1956 72
45. Tibet Medal, 1903–1904..........73
46. Zulu Rebellion, 1906................74
47. Indian General Service Medal, 1908–1935 75
48. Sudan Medal, 1910 76
49. 1914 Star 77
50. 1914–1915 Star 77
51. British War Medal, 1914–1920................................78
52. Mercantile Marine War Medal, 1914–1918 78
53. Victory Medal, 1914–1918 79
54. Territorial Force War Medal, 1914–1919................................80
55. Naval General Service Medal, 1915–1964................................81
56. General Service Medal (Army and RAF), 1918–1964..............82
57. Indian General Service Medal, 1936–1939 83
58. 1939–45 Star 84
59. Atlantic Star, 1939–1945 85
60. Air Crew Europe Star, 1939–1944................................85
61. Africa Star, 1940–1942............86
62. Pacific Star, 1941–1945...........86
63. Burma Star, 1941–1945 87
64. Italy Star, 1943–1945...............88
65. France and Germany Star, 1944–1945................................88
66. The Defence Medal, 1939–1945................................89
67. The War Medal, 1939–1945 90
68. The Korea Medal, 1950–1953 .91
69. The Campaign Service Medal, 1962 to date..................92
70. Australian and New Zealand Vietnam Service Medal, 1964–1973................................93
71. The South Atlantic Medal, 1982..94
72. The Gulf Medal, 1990–1991....95

INTRODUCTION

Naval and military medallions awarded to officers have been known in this country since the reign of Queen Elizabeth I, but the first distinction which could be won by an ordinary soldier was authorised in May 1643 by Charles I. This was an oval silver badge to be worn on the breast by those who distinguished themselves in 'forlorn hopes' and was obviously a reward for gallantry. The first award for war service was a medal issued by the Commonwealth to commemorate the Battle of Dunbar, where the Royalist Scots were defeated on 3rd September 1650. This medal, gold for officers and silver for men, was worn suspended by a chain or cord from the recipient's neck. In the ealry nineteenth century, gold crosses and medals were awarded to senior or commanding officers for services during the Peninsular campaign of the Napoleonic Wars, but it was not until 1815 that the battle of Waterloo gave birth to the modern campaign medal – that is to say a similar medal awarded to all classes and ranks, from duke to drummer boy.

'Clasp' or 'bar' is used impartially to describe a bar which bears the name or date of a campaign or action. Although clasps were first issued with the Sutlej Campaign Medal, their origin was due to the large number of battles and engagements commemorated by the Naval and Military General Service Medals, which would otherwise have necessitated the issue of dozens of separate awards. In most cases the bar is affixed by ears to the medal suspender, but occasionally it is sewn direct on to the ribbon, as, for example, with the World War II campaign stars.

Where the medal is not described as bronze or cupro-nickel it is silver. The diameter of a medal, unless otherwise stated, is always 1.42in (35mm) and the ribbon, with a similar proviso, is 1.25in (or 32mm). Widths of colour on the various ribbons are measured in fractions of an inch, or the metric scale, whichever is the more convenient. 10mm, for example, reads very awkwardly when translated into 25/64ths of an inch. Where description of the suspender is omitted, it means that suspension is by means of a plain, straight suspender pinned through a claw to the top of the medal. This suspender usually swivels, but is occasionally fixed. The 1939–45 War Medal has a typical example of a plain, straight, non-swivelling suspender.

The obverse is the face of a medal mentioned first in any catalogue and is the side which usually bears the Sovereign's head. The reverse is the side carrying the design, and often an inscription, and cannot be seen when the medal is worn.

Order of wearing for campaign medals is in chronological sequence, but according to the date of the campaign and not the issue of the medal. For example, the holder of the India General Service Medal (1908) with bar 'Waziristan 1919–21' would wear it after any awards for World War I. Until the middle of the nineteenth century there were no instructions for precedence or manner of wearing medals, and any number of permutations appear in contemporary prints, including at least one where the holder of four medals wore them on the left side of his chest, but one up, one down and one each right and left, presumably to present a balanced effect! A later regulation laid down that medals must be worn in one or two horizontal rows, and it is not uncommon to find photographs of Crimea War veterans wearing their awards in this manner; five or six medals in two rows. The custom of wearing a small piece of ribbon without the medal when in undress uniform appears to have started in India about the middle of the nineteenth century. One of the most popular misconceptions about medals appears to have originated in the early stages of World War I and is the widely held belief that a son may wear his father's medals.

Contemporary spelling has been used throughout; thus Cabul or Cabool in 1842 becomes Kabul in 1880, and Coomassie in 1874 is spelled Kumassi twenty-six years later. Early translations of Indian place names vary considerably and Bhurtphore, for instance, may also be written Burtpoor, Bhurtpoor, Burtpore, or Bhurtpore, according to taste!

WHERE TO BUY MEDALS

Every medal collector is asked at some time or another, two questions. Why do you collect medals and where do you find them? The first answer you know, otherwise you would be browsing over the collection of vintage motor cars or matchbox labels (depending on taste and/or pocket) instead of reading this book. The answer to the second question however, tends to vary. According to some collectors, during their summer holiday they have bought for a small sum rare medals casually thrown in a box/heap/tray in a dirty junk shop situated in the back street of some seaside town. Beware these delightful tales because if only half of them are true, at certain times of the year the coast resorts are full of collectors waving aloft their valuable acquisitions and yelling 'Eureka', or whatever one shouts in these circumstances. Occasionally the venue is altered to some far-flung place but the end product is always the same – something for next to nothing.

Having scoured the back streets of many towns, the only medals I saw in junk shops were usually junk and the only medal ever offered to me in the far-flung (Northern Nigeria to be precise) was such an exorbitant price that it aggravated my prickly heat. In days of old when medals were melted down for their silver content and bronze medals were thrown on the scrap heap, there were certainly some cheap buys to be made, but not for the last twenty or thirty years. Look for bargains by all means but bear in mind that many medals in junk and antique shops can be bought cheaper, and in better condition, from a reputable numismatic dealer. It is unfortunate that many collectors, especially novices, fight shy of the leading dealers. Whilst it is true that they will not give you something for nothing, certainly they will give you value for money, and if it subsequently transpires that the piece is 'wrong' your purchase money will be refunded. Small collectors grow into big collectors, and beginners with but a small sum of money to spend (a condition that afflicts most collectors from time to time) should not be deterred by an imposing address.

CLASSIFICATION AND CONDITION

Whilst the condition of a medal is sometimes a matter of opinion (buyers and sellers tend to have differing views) its worth, as with all collectable material, varies according to the rarity of the piece. To put it plainly, a knocked about World War I Victory Medal may not be given house room, whereas a fifteen bar Military General Service Medal with similar damage would be received with open arms. A realistic guide to condition reads something like this: Mint, should mean what it says, pristine condition; E.F., extremely fine, small scuff marks and minute flaws; V.F., very fine, obvious signs of wear and tear, possibly marked by contact with other medals, but no major defects; F. fine, but not fine as applied to a fine piece of porcelain but rather well worn; Fair, means fairly well battered and if some honest citizen puts Worn as a description, it may well be difficult to determine whether the item started life as a medal or a crown piece. Any permutation is possible and a medal is sometimes described as VF/EF, meaning that the obverse (always given first) is only V.F. whilst the reverse is extremely fine.

Occasionally one sees classifications such as N.E.F., meaning nearly E.F., or G.V.F. for Good Very Fine, i.e., better than V.F. but not good enough for E.F., as an attempt to give a more precise definition. In this context, the description of a medal shown as 'E.F. apart from two edge knocks' is rather like writing 'Motor car, as new, apart from two crumpled mudguards'. Similarly, an invitation to buy a medal which is 'E.F. (but once converted to a menu holder)' is similar to 'Pair of valuable short swords (have been adapted as coal tongs)'. It is a good working rule to avoid like the plague any medal which has been renamed, repaired or rehashed in any way unless it is sold for little more than the value of the silver content.

DISPLAY AND CLEANING

As a novice I was somewhat overawed by people who suggested quite elaborate methods of card indexing a collection, writing it up, display cases and so forth. It all sounded very complicated and a far cry from just collecting medals. It is, of course, a matter for the individual. A collection can be housed with special lighting, descriptive cards, etc., or, at the other extreme, it can be tumbled into the odd drawer or shoe box. The last method is certainly guaranteed not to improve the condition of any medal, but on the other hand I have seen equally cavalier treatment by people who are presumed to know better. Certainly, if nothing else, the prudent collector will wish to keep a notebook to record the price and date of purchase of his medals.

To clean or not to clean is purely a matter of personal preference. If one collector prefers medals complete with patina and suspended from aged ribbons, as opposed to another who likes shining bright medals with new ribbons, who is to say which of them is wrong? Certainly not me. Bear in mind however that some reproduction ribbons, manufactured for older medals, have been copied from faded colours and are differently woven.

THE COLLECTING FIELD

Most beginners, fascinated by the range and scope of their new hobby, usually start by collecting everything in sight – pocket permitting. However, it is not long before he, or she, begins to specialise and here the list is almost endless. A few which come to mind are a particular corps or regiment, theatre of war, campaigns, specific actions, casualties, prisoners of war, territorial associations, public school boys, nurses, war correspondents and civilians. The First World War 'Pals' battalions are also beginning to attract a great deal of attention. A number of collectors seek medals bearing their own surnames. Easy enough for Smith but rather more difficult for a Chedwyn-Smith.

Finally, never commit the cardinal sin of splitting a named group because someone has offered a good price for one of the medals in the group. You will not only throw away history but also money in the long term.

RESEARCH

Once the bug has bitten, the collector will wish to find out something about the man, probably long since dead, whose medals he now holds. Usually the best source is the Public Record Office, Ruskin Avenue, Kew, Richmond, Surrey, TW9 4DU (081 876 3444), which houses medal rolls, muster rolls, description books and various service documents. Admission is by reader's ticket which will be issued on production of proof of identity. Closed for the first two weeks in October each year. In addition, over a hundred different free leaflets, covering different fields of research, are published under the auspices of the P.R.O. These leaflets are available at Kew and at Chancery Lane, London WC2A 1LR. (081 876 3444).

The venue for research on the Imperial Indian Army is the India Office Library and Records, Orbit House, Blackfriars Road, London, SE1 8NG. (071 412 7873).

Another fruitful field is the Newspaper Library of the British Library in Colindale Avenue, London NW9 5HE (071 323 7355). On a more parochial level, County Record Offices are usually informative, especially on local regiments and units. Nor should district libraries be overlooked; they are always helpful and many of them have local newspapers on film.

Last, but by no means least, are the curators of regimental museums. The latter are always run on a tight budget so please remember to enclose a stamped, addressed envelope when making enquiries.

With the best will in the world, however, records are often incomplete, and the quest is further complicated by human error which has crept into these documents. For example, there is no record of service of either Captain Marschatik who appears in the Waterloo Medal Roll or Captain Marschalek who was eligible for the Military General Service Medal. They were in fact the same man, Captain Gustavus von Marschalk, which is the name shown in the Army List; but on his half-pay papers, signed by the man himself, the spelling is 'Marschalck'.

As with all detective work, the end product is often frustrating, sometimes sublime and occasionally ridiculous. I once spent two days wading through documents to find why a cavalryman, whose Military General Service Medal was in my possession, had been pensioned. Amid a welter of papers of men wounded by musket balls, riddled by grapeshot and slashed by swords, what terrible wound had struck down my hussar trumpeter? According to his discharge papers he 'suffered a diseased testicle as the result of a fall from his horse at Menin in 1815'. So much for the thundering hooves and flashing sabres!

ELIGIBILITY OF ACTIONS

With many campaign awards it is difficult to follow the logic which allows, or disallows, the eligibility of certain actions for medals or clasps. The bar 'Assye' on the Army of India medal is obviously justified. Wellesley's 4,000 men attacked and defeated a force more than ten times their number. The enemy, largely French officered, fought well, especially the Mahratta artillerymen who continued to serve their guns until they were bayonetted. Over a third (1,566) of the British and Indian troops were killed or wounded and the action gained a battle honour for the regiments involved; in addition to a clasp. By contrast, 'Asseerghur', on the same medal, commemorates the capture of a fort which surrendered after a bombardment lasting 55 minutes. Casualties among the attackers, according to Wellesley's despatch, amounted to one drummer and a pioneer killed and five other ranks wounded. Although there was no battle honour for the action it still merited, if that is the word, a clasp.

Compare this with Lake's capture of Agra, the legendary 'Key to Hindoostan', on 18 October 1803, at the cost of 228 casualties to the British. This victory also secured a massive amount of stores, including field guns and transport, a substantial treasure chest and 2,500 opportunists from Scindia's infantry who promptly changed over to the winning side. However, this important action gained neither battle honour nor clasp.

In more recent times fighting in the Suez Canal Zone, from 1951 to 1954, cost the lives of 60 British soldiers and over 600 wounded, but no medal, no clasp. This lack of official recognition for a difficult and dangerous posting has been raised on several occasions in Parliament. By comparison, members of the British peace keeping force who served in Lebanon, 1983–1984, were not subjected to hostile fire, nor were there any casualties. Nevertheless they were recipients of a medal and the clasp 'Lebanon'. Such examples could be repeated ad infinitum.

THE MAN BEHIND THE MEDAL

The old style collector (one of each irrespective of regiment or recipient) has long since gone and the modern enthusiast is more concerned with the man who wore the medal, rather than the medal itself. Obviously, in this context, some medals are won the hard way while others are practically served up with the rations. The Waterloo medal commemorates a bloody battle – but not for everybody. For example, officers and men of the 2/35th Foot, through no fault of their own, guarded the right flank of the Allied army and were never in action; although the regiment did have one casualty as the result of 'friendly fire'. Hence medals to the 2/35th do not command the same price as, for instance, those to the 27th Foot which was in the thick of the fighting and lost 478 out of 698 effectives.

A man, whom I knew, used to march past the Cenotaph every Remembrance Day proudly wearing his 1914 Star and bar trio. The image of a typical Old Contemptible – but not so. Early in October 1914 he strayed over the frontier into Holland where he was comfortably interned for the remainder of the war. Quite unlike Frank Richards, author of *Old Soldiers never Die*, who wore similar medals for his service in the trenches on the Western Front from August 1914 until November 1918.

In the First World War the 10th Lincolns landed in France on 9 January 1916, just too late to qualify for a 1914/15 Star. In due course the survivors received British War and Victory medals for their three years in the front line. The 34th London landed on 1 August 1918 and for a stint of nearly three months in action, as opposed to three years, its members also received a B.W.M. and Victory.

During World War II troops of the 146th Infantry Brigade served in Iceland for over two years without hearing a shot fired in anger – and after twelve months qualified for a Defence medal. The same award was earned after three years by heavy rescue workers, ambulance drivers, firemen and the like, many of whom were at the sharp end throughout the Blitz on London and other cities. Incidentally, ninety days U.K. service in a mine and bomb disposal unit also earned a Defence medal.

Perhaps these anomalies (and there are many more) are not so strange when one reflects that a committee sat in 1916 and solemnly debated whether gallantry decorations awarded for services behind the line should have different coloured ribbons to those earned for bravery in the trenches!

ODD MAN OUT

It is surprising how often medals are found named to regiments which were not present in the campaign, or battle, for which the awards were made. Similarly, the unit shown on the medal may be different to that which appears on the roll. For example, Ensign Rind is shown on the Army of India medal roll credited with the clasp 'Bhurtpore' which he apparently earned while serving with the 3rd Extra Cavalry. However, neither that unit nor his own regiment, the 20th Native Infantry, were engaged at the siege. One can only assume that Ensign Rind was temporarily detached on other duties.

A similar situation arises in the case of officers who took leave in order to participate in some promising Victorian campaign in which their own battalion was not engaged. Thus Lieut. Rybot's 1904 Tibet medal shows his own regiment, the 28th Punjabis, which never entered Tibet. In fact Rybot served in the Younghusbandman expedition as a volunteer with the Mounted Infantry.

Quite often, in the case of other ranks, 'the odd man out' will be an officer's servant or a specialist. George Dolby's 1854 Indian General Service medal, bar 'Chin Lushai 1889–90', shows him to be a gunner in the Royal Horse Artillery, which was not involved in the Burma campaign. The mystery is solved by a medal roll which reveals that Dolby was attached to the Government Telegraph Department and accompanied the Chittagong column as a signaller.

This specialist notion may also account for similar oddities in later wars. Moving forward into the 20th century, and the Great War, it is impossible (at least in theory) to find medals to the Northern Cyclist Battalion or the Huntingtonshire Cyclist Battalion. These formations remained in the United Kingdom and neither served abroad as a complete unit. Nevertheless, British War and Victory medals have been recorded to both battalions. The naming reads, 'N. Cyc. Bn.' or 'Hunts. Cyc. Bn.' as the case may be.

CASUALTIES

Medals to casualties, whereby the man's whereabouts is precisely pinpointed, have always held a fascination for collectors. Unfortunately the cost of medals to earlier casualties, because of the relatively small numbers involved, requires fairly deep pockets. The charge of the Light Brigade at Balaclava, 113 killed and 165 wounded out of a total of 673 sabres is an example. Therefore there is a growing tendency to concentrate on the largest group of named awards, namely those for the Great War.

Dealing first with the Royal Navy, which lost 32,208 officers and ratings at sea. The most expensive medals are generally those to 'Q' ship casualties or submarines. These are followed by any ship to ship encounter; for instance H.M. ships *Partridge* and *Pellew* versus four German destroyers, in 1917. Lower down the scale are fleet actions; Dogger Bank, Coronel, Jutland, etc., and then lives lost as the result of torpedoing, usually by U-boats. The cheapest are medals to those unfortunates killed when their vessel struck a mine, or possibly just disappeared.

The four British warships, each destroyed by an internal explosion, are in a separate category. Probably the most famous of these is H.M.S. *Bulwark*, an old battleship, which blew up at Sheerness on 15 November 1914 with the loss of 738 officers and men. An Admiralty Court enquiry could not find a reason for the disaster and sabotage has always been suspected. Sheerness Harbour was also the venue for a second calamity when *Princess Irene*, an auxiliary minelayer, was undergoing repairs. At 11.15 a.m. on 27 May 1915, when 78 dockyard workmen, 30 officers and 23 ratings were on board, a tremendous explosion virtually blew the ship apart. Only one workman and a few seamen survived.

H.M.S. *Natal*, an armoured cruiser, was another sabotage suspect. On 30 December 1915 she was lying in Cromarty harbour when fire broke out on the ship. Within a short time her after magazines exploded and she sank almost immediately. 405 of her crew, out of a complement of 704, were killed. The fourth ill-fated vessel was a dreadnought, H.M.S. *Vanguard* a Jutland veteran, lying at anchor in Scapa Flow. On 9 July 1917 she blew up with the loss of nearly every man on board. Only two seamen survived out of a crew of 670.

Turning to the Merchant Navy, the dead of the British Mercantile Marine totalled 14,661. Although many of these men were lost when cargo boats and tramp steamers were sunk there were also some famous, or rather infamous, sinkings. Probably the best known is the S.S. *Lusitania*, a Cunard liner of over 30,000 tons. At 2.15 p.m. on 7 May 1915, when the ship was ten miles south of the Old Head of Kinsale, she was struck nearly amidships by a torpedo fired from U.20. This was followed by a second explosion which may have occurred in the engine room. Eleven minutes later the liner foundered. Of those on board no fewer than 1,198 passengers and crew were drowned. Following hostile reports in the American Press, the Germans struck a commemorative medal which showed the *Lusitania* carrying war material (and was thus a legitimate target). This was rebutted by the British in a leaflet (***see figure 1***), which was sold, together with a copy of the medallion, for the benefit of St. Dunstan's.

Insofar as the British Army is concerned, it sustained a higher casualty rate, pro rata ration strength, than either of the other two Services. Unfortunately the classic *Soldiers Died in the Great War 1914–19* published by H.M.S.O. does not differentiate between those soldiers killed on the Western Front and those slain in Italy. In addition, most of the casualties listed under Egypt were usually killed in Palestine, sometimes Syria, occasionally Libya, but rarely Egypt. The following table specifies the theatre of war and the totals include both officers and other ranks.

Theatre of War	*Killed or Died of Wounds*	*Missing and Prisoners of War*
France and Flanders	416,617	295,318
Dardanelles	16,580	7,525
Mesopotamia	16,389	15,221
Palestine, and adjacent territory (includes Dominion troops)	10,187	3,871
Macedonia	4,096	2,778
East Africa (includes Dominion troops)	3,443	1,301
Italy	1,288	344
South West Africa	246*	782
North Russia	211	177
Ireland (1916 Uprising)	103	Nil
Siberia	less than 100	?
North China	20	Nil
Aden	18	Nil
Malaya	6	Nil

*All Dominion.

(Mutiny of Indian 5th Light Infantry: 13 men of the Singapore Volunteer Rifles were also killed)

India, North West Frontier: hundreds of casualties, but mostly to Indian regiments or the South Waziristan Militia. Very few British.

The above figures are British Army casualties and do not include Empire troops, unless indicated.

Comparing casualty totals for the Western Front and Italy it is obvious that the scarcity factor for a man K.I.A. in Italy, as against France and Flanders, is in the region of 1 to 323. Thus, medals to a soldier killed in Italy should be scarcer and accordingly dearer. Generally this is true, but it does not take into account the emotive feelings connected with some of the famous battles on the Western Front. The best known of these is probably the first day of the Battle of the Somme. At 7.30 a.m. on 1 July 1916, fifteen British Divisions went over the top to attack the German trenches. By nightfall, 19,240 officers and men were dead, or died of wounds, 35,493 wounded, 2,152 missing (missing on the Western Front was usually synonymous with being blown to bits) and 585 were prisoners of war. The cream of Kitchener's volunteer army had been destroyed.

Naval personnel also fought on land. In 1914, following the mobilization of reserves, the Admiralty, probably for the first time in history, had more men than were needed for sea service. The result was the formation of the Royal Naval Division, comprising three brigades. The 1st consisted of the Collingwood, Hawke, Benbow and Drake battalions, the 2nd comprised the Howe, Hood, Anson and Nelson battalions, whilst four Royal Marine Light Infantry battalions, titled Portsmouth, Plymouth, Chatham and Deal, made up the 3rd. The Division eventually fought on four Fronts and the following totals include both officers and other ranks.

Theatre of War	*Killed or Died of Wounds*	*Prisoners of War or Interned*
Antwerp (Belgium 1914)	58	2,371
Dardenelles (1915)	2,253	2
Salonika (1916) 3rd Brigade only: no figures available.		
Western Front (1916–18)	7,820	2,830

In May 1916 the Division sailed for France to become part of the British Expeditionary Force. As the result of casualties sustained in the Dardenelles campaign, the sailors were re-formed into two brigades, each of four battalions. The 188th Brigade: 1st and 2nd Royal Marines, Anson and Hood, and the 189th Brigade: Hawke, Drake, Howe and Nelson. The formation was re-titled the 63rd (RN) Division and brought up to strength with the addition of an infantry brigade – the 190th. Thus totals for 1916–18 include a proportion of army casualties.

The junior Service, the Royal Flying Corps, expanded from 1,100 (all ranks) in August 1914 to 144,078 by March 1918. However, as far as casualties are concerned, various official lists have been differently computed and thus give different final figures; but all the returns show a total in the region of 8,000 – killed, wounded and missing. April 1917 to March 1918 features as the worst year for flying casualties; 2,097 airmen were reported killed or missing over the Western Front alone.

Statistics for the Royal Naval Air Service which, together with the R.F.C. was incorporated into the newly-formed Royal Air Force on 1 April 1918, are partially concealed in R.N. casualty lists. R.N.A.S. personnel not only flew, but also manned armoured cars in places as far apart as Belgium in 1914, Gallipoli 1915 and Russia 1916/17.

Prisoners of War. Rolls held by the War Information Bureau in London were largely destroyed during the 1940 Blitz. However, a complete list of British officers of all three Services taken prisoner between August 1914 and November 1918, and culled from the records of Cox & Company, the banking house, was published in 1988. In addition, an Enquiry List 1917 from the British Red Cross and Order of St. John, reprinted in 1989, gives the names and units of over 25,000 British and Empire personnel. Both volumes are available from the Naval and Military Press Ltd., 1 Old Bond Street, London WC1X 3TD (071 499 5022).

The P.R.O. has rolls of British and Dominion P.O.W.s (mostly army) held in Germany, Turkey and Switzerland in 1916 contained in AIR 1/892/204/5 and 696/7 and 8. A list of British Army and Dominion prisoners in German camps in July 1915 may be found in ADM 1/8420/124.

MINIATURES

Miniature medals, once only seen with mess dress, are now often worn on evening dress, dinner jackets, or even lounge suits on certain occasions. Despite the fact that various medal societies have flourishing miniature medal sections, no regulation has ever been traced which authorises miniatures to be worn. The first miniature apparently dates from the immediate post-Waterloo period when small replicas of the Waterloo Medal were worn as a form of jewellery by wives, whose officer husbands had been present at the battle. Officers actually wearing miniature medals in undress uniform were first photographed soon after the Crimean War.

Although most miniatures are 18mm in diameter, as against 35mm for a standard medal, there are also semi-miniatures of different sizes on the market. Some of these are almost as large as the full size original, which rather negates the purpose of a miniature. Named miniatures, especially those with provenance, are something of a rarity and command a commensurate price.

Royal approval for the award of 67 naval clasps to the British War medal was granted in 1920, but the issue was abandoned on the grounds of cost. However, some Royal Navy personnel, chiefly officers, had the full size and miniature clasps manufactured at their own expense. A typical example is shown at ***figure 2***, although it should be noted that no one man could have gained such a wide range of bars.

MEDAL RELATED COLLECTABLES

Obvious candidates under this heading are copies of discharge documents, medal rolls and letters written from a theatre of war. There is, however, a great deal of other related material which is often available.

The aftermath of the Battle of Waterloo was the first occasion when prize money was separately paid to an individual soldier, or his next of kin, instead of in bulk to a regimental agent. ***Figure 3*** shows a Waterloo prize money certificate in favour of former Sergeant Lewis Nolte, 1st Light Battalion, King's German Legion (part of the British Army since 1812). The money was duly paid in 1817 at Hanover where Nolte lived after his discharge from the army in 1816.

The First World War also spawned a number of 'firsts'. Brown paper envelopes (normally blank) in which medals were sent carried printed explicit directions on how the medals should be worn in the case of merchant seamen. ***See figures 4 and 5***.

Another innovation was the facsimile letter from King George V which was handed to each returning prisoner of war at his reception station (***figure 6***). A similar letter from the monarch was given to World War II returnees. Furthermore, at least three regimental committees were instrumental in the gift of 'welcome home' medallions to their homecoming P.O.W.s and the Queen's Regiment offering is illustrated at ***figures 7 and 8***. These were meant to be worn (but rarely were) on the watch chain. In fact they were not well received as the recipients were usually loth to advertise their captivity in enemy hands.

In addition to the deceased's medals, next of kin received a memorial scroll and a bronze plaque both named to the fallen. The example shown at ***figure 9*** is to an aircraftsman in the R.A.F. After World War II a similar scroll, but without a plaque, was sent to the closest relative of a dead serviceman (or woman). The Second World War scroll, also to an airman, is depicted at ***figure 10***.

The armed forces have printed forms for practically every eventuality, including notification of death, and the form used by the army in World War I was numbered B.104. This usually stated that the deceased had been killed in action or died of wounds in his Country's service. Thus the next of kin might visualise the dead man bravely falling in the heat of battle. Such consolation was not available to the mother who received the B.104, illustrated at ***figure 11***, which bore the callous message that her son had 'Died from dysentery in a railway truck' in Northern France.

Please do not destroy this

When you have read it carefully through kindly pass it on to a friend.

A

German Naval Victory

"With joyful pride we contemplate this latest deed of our navy. . . ."—
Kölnische Volkszeitung, 10th May, 1915.

This medal has been struck in Germany with the object of keeping alive in German hearts the recollection of the glorious achievement of the German Navy in deliberately destroying an unarmed passenger ship, together with 1,198 non-combatants, men, women and children.

On the obverse, under the legend "No contraband" *(Keine Bannware)*, there is a representation of the *Lusitania* sinking. The designer has put in guns and aeroplanes, which (as was certified by United States Government officials after inspection) the *Lusitania* did *not* carry; but has conveniently omitted to put in the women and children, which the world knows she *did* carry.

On the reverse, under the legend "Business above all" *(Geschäft über alles)* the figure of Death sits at the booking office of the Cunard Line [illegible] out tickets to passengers, who refuse to attend to the warning against submarines given by a German. This picture seeks apparently to propound the theory that if a murderer warns his victim of his intention, the guilt of the crime will rest with the victim, not with the murderer.

Replicas of the medal are issued by the Lusitania Souvenir Medal Committee, 32, Duke Street, Manchester Square W. 1.
All profits accruing to this Committee will be handed to St. Dunstan's Blinded Soldiers and Sailors Hostel.

Figures 1 and 2

Figure 3

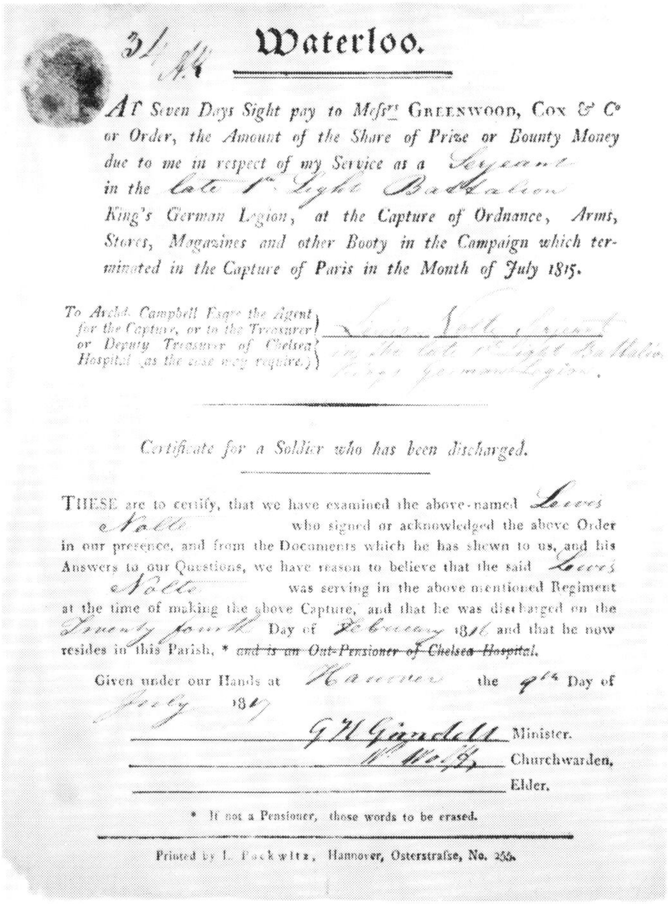

Waterloo.

3/4 N.4

AT Seven Days Sight pay to Messrs. GREENWOOD, COX & Co or Order, the Amount of the Share of Prize or Bounty Money due to me in respect of my Service as a Sergeant in the late 1st Light Battalion King's German Legion, at the Capture of Ordnance, Arms, Stores, Magazines and other Booty in the Campaign which terminated in the Capture of Paris in the Month of July 1815.

To Archd. Campbell Esqre. the Agent for the Captors, or to the Treasurer or Deputy Treasurer of Chelsea Hospital (as the case may require.)

Louis Nolte Sergeant in the late 1st Light Battalion Kings German Legion.

Certificate for a Soldier who has been discharged.

THESE are to certify, that we have examined the above-named Louis Nolte who signed or acknowledged the above Order in our presence, and from the Documents which he has shewn to us, and his Answers to our Questions, we have reason to believe that the said Louis Nolte was serving in the above mentioned Regiment at the time of making the above Capture, and that he was discharged on the Twenty fourth Day of February 1816 and that he now resides in this Parish, * ~~and is an Out-Pensioner of Chelsea Hospital.~~

Given under our Hands at Hanover the 9th Day of July 1817

G H Gjandell Minister.

Wm Wolf Churchwarden,

Elder.

* If not a Pensioner, those words to be erased.

Printed by L. Packwitz, Hannover, Osterstrafse, No. 255.

Figures 4 and 5

BRITISH WAR MEDAL

— Issued to —

The Mercantile Marine.

This medal should be worn on the left breast with the King's head showing.

When worn with the Mercantile Marine War Medal it must be next to the *Green* strip (that is: the Mercantile Marine War Medal must be the nearer to the left arm).

Mercantile Marine War Medal.

This Medal should be worn on the left breast with the King's head showing.

The red strip of the riband should be nearest the left arm.

BOARD OF TRADE.

BUCKINGHAM PALACE

1918.

The Queen joins me in welcoming you on your release from the miseries & hardships, which you have endured with so much patience & courage.

During these many months of trial, the early rescue of our gallant Officers & Men from the cruelties of their captivity has been uppermost in our thoughts.

We are thankful that this longed for day has arrived, & that back in the old Country you will be able once more to enjoy the happiness of a home & to see good days among those who anxiously look for your return.

George R.I.

Figure 6

Figures 7 and 8

Figure 9

HE whom this scroll commemorates was numbered among those who, at the call of King and Country, left all that was dear to them, endured hardness, faced danger, and finally passed out of the sight of men by the path of duty and self-sacrifice, giving up their own lives that others might live in freedom.

Let those who come after see to it that his name be not forgotten.

A.C./II William Taylor
Royal Air Force

This scroll commemorates

Pilot Officer W. G. Scarlett
Royal Air Force

held in honour as one who served King and Country in the world war of 1939-1945 and gave his life to save mankind from tyranny. May his sacrifice help to bring the peace and freedom for which he died.

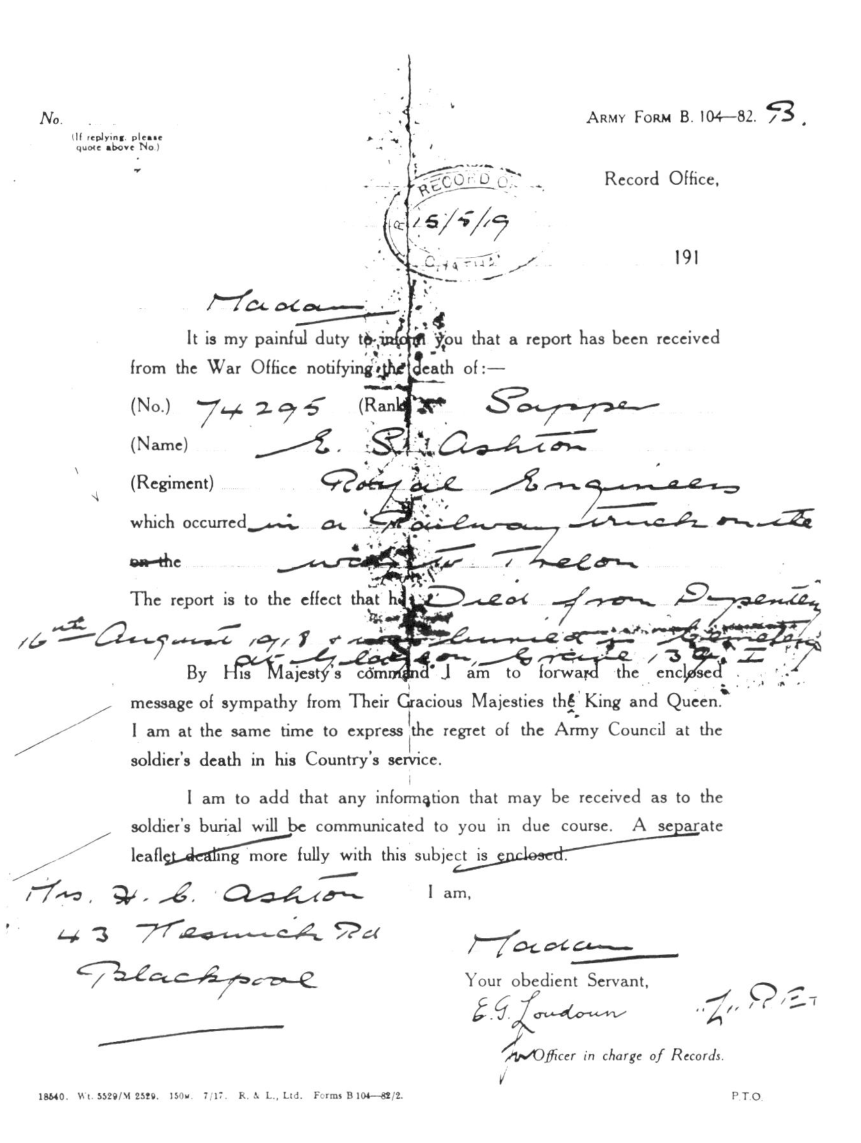
No. (If replying, please quote above No.)

ARMY FORM B. 104—82. B.

Record Office, 15/5/19

191

Madam,

It is my painful duty to inform you that a report has been received from the War Office notifying the death of:—

(No.) 74295 (Rank) Sapper

(Name) E. S. Ashton

(Regiment) Royal Engineers

which occurred in a Railway truck on the way to Thelon

The report is to the effect that he Died from Dysentery 16th August 1918 & was buried at Gladson Grave 139. I

By His Majesty's command I am to forward the enclosed message of sympathy from Their Gracious Majesties the King and Queen. I am at the same time to express the regret of the Army Council at the soldier's death in his Country's service.

I am to add that any information that may be received as to the soldier's burial will be communicated to you in due course. A separate leaflet dealing more fully with this subject is enclosed.

Mrs. H. C. Ashton
43 Keswick Rd
Blackpool

I am,

Madam

Your obedient Servant,

E. G. Loudoun

Officer in charge of Records.

18840. Wt. 5529/M 2529. 150M. 7/17. R. & L., Ltd. Forms B 104—82/2.

P.T.O.

Figure 11

Figure 10

DIRECTORY

WHERE TO MEET OTHER COLLECTORS

Every collector benefits by contacts with kindred souls, whether it be exchange of information, swopping duplicates, or just chatting about aspects of the hobby. The largest society in the United Kingdom is The Orders and Medals Research Society whose membership secretary is N.I. Brooks, 21 Colonels Lane, Chertsey, Surrey KT16 8RH. In addition to holding meetings, the Society also publishes a hefty quarterly journal, packed with information and well worth the subscription fee. There are branches in Scotland, Manchester, Cheltenham and Sussex and overseas branches in Hong Kong, Canada and Australia. The parent Society also has two thriving sections, one for collectors of miniatures and one for ribbon enthusiasts.

The other U.K. society which caters solely for medal collectors is The Birmingham Medal Society, secretary J.P. Wilson, 10 Edward Street, Milverton, Leamington Spa, CV32 6AX.

Some of the other societies in English-speaking countries are as follows: THE ORDERS AND MEDALS SOCIETY OF AMERICA, secretary: John E. Lelle, P.O. Box 484,Glassboro, New Jersey 08028 U.S.A. MILITARY COLLECTORS CLUB OF CANADA, secretary: G. Fairless, 15 Abel Place, St. Albert, Alberta T8N 2Z5, Canada. THE MILITARY MEDAL SOCIETY OF SOUTH AFRICA, contact Gordon Bickley, 1 Jacqueline Avenue, Northcliff, South Africa 2195.

WHERE TO SEE BRITISH CAMPAIGN MEDALS

The following guide to places where campaign medals are on view to the public is arranged alphabetically by location, and not by regimental title. Visiting hours may vary considerably between seasons and there are a number of museums which admit visitors only by appointment, or are closed during the winter. These are marked respectively (BAO) or (CW). Hence, before making a long journey, it is wise to verify dates and times with the curator by letter or telephone. I apologise in advance to museums with medal displays which are not mentioned.

England:

ALDERSHOT. Army Physical Training Corps Museum, Corps Depot, Queen's Avenue, GU11 2LB. (0252 347 131) (BAO) for afternoons and weekends.

Queen Alexandra's Royal Army Nursing Corps Museum, RHQ, Royal Pavilion, Farnborough Road, GU11 1PZ. (0252 349 315)

Royal Army Dental Corps Museum, Headquarters RADC, Evelyn Woods Road. (0252 24431 Ext 2782).

Royal Army Medical Corps Historical Museum, Keogh Barracks, Ash Vale, near Aldershot, Hants. GU12 5RQ. (0252 24431 ext Keogh 5212). Excellent display, including a photograph of Surgeon Manley's decorations; the only man entitled to a Victoria Cross and the Iron Cross.

Regimental Museum Royal Corps of Transport, RHQ RCT, Buller Barracks, GU11 2BX. (0252 348 837).

ALNWICK. The Fifth or Royal Northumberland Fusiliers Regimental Museum, The Abbot's Tower, Alnwick Castle, Northumberland NE66 1NG. (0665 602 152). (CW).

BAGSHOT. Museum of the Royal Army Chaplains' Department, Bagshot Park, Surrey GU19 5PL. (0276 71717 Ext 2845) (BAO).

BERWICK UPON TWEED. King's Own Scottish Borderers Museum, The Barracks, Northumberland TD15 1DG. (0289 307 426)

BLACKBURN. East Lancashire Regimental Museum, in a gallery in Blackburn Museum, Museum Street, Lancs BB1 7AJ. (0254 667 130). Includes 5th Lancashire Militia and local rifle volunteers.

BLANDFORD FORUM. Royal Signals Museum, Blandford Camp, near Blandford Forum, Dorset DT11 8RH. (0258 482248). The Corps medal collection in addition to army communications.

BODMIN. The Duke of Cornwall's Light Infantry Regimental Museum, The Keep, Cornwall PL31 1EG. (0208 72810). Excellent medal display.

BOVINGTON. Royal Armoured Corps and Royal Tank Museums, Bovington Camp, near Wareham, Dorset BH20 6JG. (0929 403 463).

BURY. Regimental Museum XX The Lancashire Fusiliers, Wellington Barracks, Lancs. (061 764 2208).

BURY ST. EDMUNDS. Suffolk Regimental Museum, The Keep, Gibraltar Barracks, Out Risbygate Street, Suffolk IP33 3RN. (0284 752394). Weekends (BAO). Excellent medal display.

CAMBERLEY. National Army Museum, Royal Military Academy Sandhurst, Surrey GU15 4PQ. Exhibits, including medals, relating to troops of the Honourable East India Company and the Imperial Indian Army, housed in the Indian Army Memorial Room. (BAO). *Written* application with at least seven days' notice.

Royal Army Ordnance Corps Museum, RAOC Training Centre, Blackdown Barracks, Deepcut, Surrey GU16 6RW. (0252 340 515/6).

CANTERBURY. The Buffs Regimental Museum,The Royal Museum, 18 High Street, Kent CT1 2JE. (0227 452 747). An impressive collection of medals with many interesting groups.

CARLISLE. The Border Regiment & King's Own Royal Border Regiment Museum, Queen Mary's Tower, The Castle, Cumbria CA3 8UR. (0228 32774).

CHATHAM. Royal Engineers Museum, Brompton Barracks, Kent ME4 4UG. (0634 406 397). Splendid display of medals.

CHELMSFORD. Essex Regimental Museum, part of the Chelmsford and Essex Museum, Oaklands Park, Moulsham Street, Essex CM2 9AQ. (0245 260 614).

CHESTER. Cheshire Military Museum, The Castle, CH1 2DN. (0244 327 617). Embraces 5th Royal Inniskilling Dragoon Guards, 3rd Carabiniers, Cheshire Yeomanry and the Cheshire Regiment.

CHICHESTER. Corps of Royal Military Police, Roussillon Barracks, Sussex PO19 4BN. (0243 786 311). New medal room added in 1991.

COLNE. British in India Museum, Sun Street, Lancs. BB8 0JJ. (0282 63129). All aspects of British rule in India including some medals. Check days and hours of visiting.

DERBY. Regimental Museum of the 9th/12th Royal Lancers (Prince of Wales'), part of Derby City Museum, The Strand, DE1 1BS. (0332 255 581). Some medals.

DONCASTER. King's Own Yorkshire Light Infantry Regimental Gallery, housed in Doncaster Museum, Chequer Road, South Yorkshire DN1 2AE. Covers local Yeomanry, Militia, Volunteer and Territorial units.Some medals. (0302 734 287).

DORCHESTER. Dorset Military Museum, The Keep, Dorset DT1 1RN. (0305 264 066). Covers the Queen's Own Dorset Yeomanry, the Dorset Regiment, Devon & Dorset Regiment, Dorset Militia and Dorset Volunteers. 1,500 medals on display.

DURHAM. Durham Light Infantry Museum, Aykley Heads, Durham City DH1 5TU. (091 384 2214). Also covers the 106th Bombay Light Infantry (later the 2nd Bn. D.L.I.) and local Militia and Volunteers. Over 1,200 medals on show.

EASTBOURNE. Sussex Combined Services Museum, Redoubt Fortress, Royal Parade, Sussex BN22 7AQ. (0323 410 300). The Royal Sussex Regiment, The Queen's Royal Irish Hussars and all yeomanry, territorial, militia and volunteer units of Sussex.

EXETER. The Devonshire Regiment, Wyvern Barracks, Barrack Road, Devon EX2 6AE.

GLOUCESTER. Regiments of Gloucestershire Museum, Gloucester Docks, GL1 2HE. (0452 22682). Combines the collections of the Gloucestershire Regiments and the Royal Gloucestershire Hussars.

GRANTHAM. 17th/21st Lancers Regimental Museum, Belvoir Castle, Lincolnshire NG33 7TJ. (0476 67413 Ext 3252). Sundays only in March and October.

GUILDFORD. The Queen's Royal Surrey Regiment Museum, Clandon Park, West Clandon, GU4 7RQ. Also embraces the Queen's Royal Regiment and the East Surrey Regiment. (0483 223419) (CW).

HALIFAX. The Duke of Wellington's Regimental Museum, housed in Bankfield Museum, Akroyd Park, HX3 6HG. (0422 354823).

HITCHIN. Hertfordshire Yeomanry & Artillery Historical Trust Museum, Hitchin Museum, Paynes Park, Herts. SG5 1EQ. Some medals. (0462 34476).

LANCASTER. King's Own Royal Regiment (Lancaster), in the City Museum, Market Square, Lancs. LA1 1HT (0524 64637). Medals include three V.C.s and a George Cross.

LEICESTER. Royal Leicestershire Regimental Museum, The Magazine, The Newarke.

(0533 554 100). Housed in the 14th century gateway.

LICHFIELD. Museum of the Staffordshire Regiment (The Prince of Wales'), Whittington Barracks, Staffs. WS14 9PY (0543 433 333 Ext 3240). Medal display includes eight of the thirteen V.C.s to men of the regiment.

LINCOLN. Museum of Lincolnshire Life, Old Barracks, Burton Road, LN1 3LY. (0522 528 448). Royal Lincolnshire Regiment and the Lincolnshire Yeomanry.

LIVERPOOL. Museum of the King's Regiment (Liverpool), within Liverpool Museum, William Brown Street, L3 8EN. (051 207 0001).

LONDON. Guards Museum, Wellington Barracks, Birdcage Walk, SW1E 6HQ. (071 414 3271). Closed on Fridays and some ceremonial days. Displays of the five regiments of Foot Guards.

Honourable Artillery Company, Armoury House, City Road, EC1 2BQ. Some medals. Intending visitors apply in *writing* at least 48 hours in advance.

Imperial War Museum, Lambeth Road, SE1 6HZ. Mainly post-1914 as far as awards and medals are concerned.

Inns of Court and City Yeomanry Museum, 10 Stone Buildings, Lincoln's Inn, WC2A 3TG. Some medals. (081 405 8112) (BAO).

Middlesex Regimental Museum, Bruce Castle, Lordship Lane, Tottenham, N17 8NU. (081 808 8772).

National Army Museum, Royal Hospital Road, Chelsea, SW3 4HT. History of the British Army from 1485. (071 730 0717).

National Maritime Museum, Greenwhich, SE10 9NF. (081 858 4422). Collectors may grieve at the sight of 120 Naval General Service medals, and their clasps, incorporated in a large silver tray. Poor lighting in the medal room.

Royal Artillery Regimental Museum, Old Royal Military Academy, Red Lion Lane, SE18 4DN. (081 854 2242 Ext 3128). Very good museum in three main rooms. (Closed at weekends).

The Royal Fusiliers Museum, H.M. Tower of London, EC3N 4AB. (071 488 5610). Another excellent museum.

Royal Hospital Museum, Royal Hospital Road, Chelsea, SW3 4SL. (071 730 0161 Ext 203). Medals and uniforms of Pensioners who have lived in the Hospital over the past 300 years.

LUTON. Bedfordshire & Hertfordshire Regimental Museum, housed in Luton Museum, Wardown Park, Beds. LU2 7HA. (0582 36941).

MAIDSTONE. The Queen's Own Royal West Kent Regiment, within Maidstone Museum, St. Faith's Street, Kent, ME14 1LH. (0622 754 497). Includes exhibits of the 20th county of London battalions, Kent Cyclists battalion and the West Kent Militia.

NEWCASTLE. 15th/19th The King's Royal Hussars and the Northumberland Hussars, housed in John George Joicey Museum, City Road, Newcastle-upon-Tyne. (091 232 4562).

NORTHAMPTON. Museum of the Northamptonshire Regiment, in Abington Park Museum, Abington. (0604 35412).

NORWICH. Royal Norfolk Regimental Museum, Shirehall, Market Avenue, NR1 31Q. (0603 223 649).

NOTTINGHAM. Sherwood Foresters Museum, The Castle, NG1 6EL. (0602 785 516). Interesting display includes a campaign medal awarded to a goat.

OXFORD. Regimental Museum Oxfordshire and Buckinghamshire Light Infantry, TA Centre, Slade Park, Headington, OX3 7JL. (0865 716 060 Ext 128). Includes the Queen's Own Oxfordshire Hussars. Over 1,800 medals on display.

PENRITH. Westmoreland & Cumberland Yeomanry Museum, Dalemain, near Penrith, Cumbria. (07684 86450) (CW).

PORTSMOUTH. Royal Navy Museum, HM Naval Base, Hampshire PO1 3LR. (0705 733 060). Excellent collection of medals displayed in campaign order.

PRESTON. Regimental Museum, Loyal Regiment (North Lancashire), Fulwood Barracks, PR2 4AA. (0772 716 543 Ext 2362).

Lancashire County & Regimental Museum, Stanley Street, PR1 4YP. (0772 264 075). East, South and Loyal North Lancashire Regiments, 14th/ 20th King's Hussars, Queen's Lancashire Regiment, Duke of Lancaster's Own Yeomanry and the Lancashire Hussars Yeomanry. A number of medal balconies.

RICHMOND, Yorkshire. The Green Howards Museum, Trinity Church Square, DL10 4QN. (0748 822133). Closed December & January. Includes Alexandra, Princess of Wales' Own Yorkshire Regiment and local Militia units and North York Rifle Volunteers. 3,000 medals including a VC and GC exhibition.

ROTHERHAM. The York and Lancaster Regimental Museum, housed in Central Library, Walker Place, South Yorkshire S65 1JH.

(0709 382 121 Ext 3625). Revolving medal display which includes nine Victoria Cross groups.

SALISBURY. Museum of the Duke of Edinburgh's Royal Regiment (Berkshire and Wiltshire), 58 The Close, Wiltshire SP1 2EX. (0722 44536). Closed December and January.

SHREWSBURY. TheShropshire Regimental Museum, The Castle, Shropshire SY1 2AT. (0743 358 516). Incorporates the King's Shropshire Light Infantry (both regular and territorial) and all Shropshir yeomanry, militia and volunteers.

SOUTHSEA. Royal Marines Museum, RM Barracks, Eastney, Portsmouth, Hamts. PO4 9PX. (0705 819385). Splendid display of all ten Royal Marine V.C.s and over 6,000 gallantry and campaign awards.

STAFFORD. 16th/5th The Queen's Royal Lancers & Staffordshire Yeomanry (QORR) Regimental Museum, Kitchener House, Lammascote Road, ST16 3TA. (0785 45840 Ext 4519). 16th Lancers, 5th Royal Irish Lancers and yeomanry.

TAUNTON. Somerset Military Museum, County Museum, The Castle, Somerset TA1 4AA. (0823 255 504). Somerset Light Infantry (Prince Albert's), North Somerset Yeomanry, West Somerset Yeomanry, Somerset Militia and Rifle Volunteer Corps. Excellent medal gallery.

TONBRIDGE. Kent and Sharpshooters Yeomanry Museum, Hever Castle, near Tonbridge, Kent TN8 7NG. (CW). East Kent Yeomanry, West Kent Yeomanry and the 3rd/4th County of London Yeomanry (Sharpshooters).

WARRINGTON. The Queen's Lancashire Regiment, Peninsular Barracks, Cheshire WA2 7BR. (0925 33563). Mornings only. Lancashire and South Lancashire Regiment Division. Separate arms and medals room.

WARWICK. Regimental Museum of the Queen's Own Hussars, The Lord Leycester Hospital, High Street, CV34 4EW. (0926 492 755). 3rd King's Own Hussars and 7th Queen's Own Hussars. Some medals.

Royal Warwickshire Regimental Museum, St. John's House, CV34 4NF. (0926 491 653). Large display of medals.

WINCHESTER. The Light Infantry Museum, Peninsular Barracks, Romsey Road, SO23 8TS. (0962 885 522 Ext 5130). Post-1968 displays only.

The Royal Green Jackets Museum, also housed in Peninsular Barracks. (0962 863 846). The Oxfordshire and Buckinghamshire Light Infantry, The King's Royal Rifle Corps and the Rifle Brigade. A truly outstanding display of some 7,000 medals including 33 Victoria Crosses. Also several unique groups and a Naval General Service medal to the 95th.

Royal Hussars Museum, same building. (0962 863 751). The 10th Royal Hussars, 11th Hussars (PAO) and Royal Hussars.

The Gurkha Museum is also located in Peninsular Barracks. (0962 842 832).

The Royal Hampshire Regiment Museum, Serle's House, Southgate Street, Hampshire SO23 9EG. (0962 863 658). Some interesting long groups.

WINDSOR. The Household Cavalry Museum, Combermere Barracks, Berkshire. (0753 868 222 Ext 5203). 1st and 2nd Life Guards, The Life Guards, Royal Horse Guards (The Blues), 1st Royal Dragoons and the Blues and Royals. Probably one of the richest and best displayed military collections.

WORCESTER. Worcestershire Regimental Museum, City Museum, Foregate Street, WR1 1DT. (0905 25371). Includes all Militia and Volunteer units of the regiment.

YORK.The Prince of Wales' Own Regiment of Yorkshire Museum, 3A Tower Street, YO1 1SB. (0904 642038). The West Yorkshire and East Yorkshire Regiments.

4th/7th Royal Dragoon Guards Museum, No 3 Tower Street, YO1 1SB. (0904 642036). Some medals.

Scotland:

ABERDEEN. Gordon Highlanders Regimental Museum, Regimental H.Q., Viewfield Road. (0224 318 174). Sunday and Wednesday afternoons otherwise (BAO).

DUNKELD. The Scottish Horse Museum, The Cross. (CW). Collection covering the period 1900–1956 includes medals.

EDINBURGH. The Royal Scots Regiment, The Castle, EH1 2YT.

Royal Scots Dragoon Guards (Royal Scots Greys) museum, housed in The Castle.

Scottish United Services Museum is also located in The Castle. (031 225 7534 Ext 400). No medals but a magnificent collection of uniforms, books and prints covering all the Scottish regiments regular, yeomanry, militia and volunteers.

FORT GEORGE. Regimental Museum of Queen's Own Highlanders, Fort George, Inverness-shire. Seaforth Highlanders and Queen's Own Cameron Highlanders. Unique collection including items from The Lovat Scouts, militia, volunteers and territorials.

GLASGOW. Museum of the Royal Highland Fusiliers, 518 Sauchiehall Street, G2 3LW. (041 332 0961). The Royal Scots Fusiliers and the Highland Light Infantry.

HAMILTON. Regimental Museum, The Cameronians (Scottish Rifles), Moe Hill, off Muir Street, Lanarkshire ML3 6BY. (0698 428 688).

PERTH. The Black Watch Museum, Balhousie Castle, Perth (on the North Inch) PH1 5HS. (0738 21281 Ext 8530).

STIRLING. Regimental Museum Argyll & Sutherland Highlanders, Stirling Castle, FK8 1EJ. (0786 75165).

Wales:

BRECON. Regimental Museum of the South Wales Borderers and Monmouthshire Regiment of the Royal Regiment of Wales, The Barracks, Powys LD3 7EB. (0874 3111 Ext 2310). Separate medal room houses more than 2,000 medals.

CAERNARVON. Regimental Museum The Royal Welch Fusiliers, The Queen's Tower, Caernarvon Castle. Museum occupies all three floors of the Tower. A large display of medals which includes the ten V.C.s of the Regiment.

CARDIFF. The Welch Regiment of the Royal Regiment of Wales, The Black and Barbican Towers, Cardiff Castle, CF1 2RB. (0222 229 367). The Welch Regiment and associated territorials, militia and volunteers. Also the first 20 years of the Royal Regiment of Wales.

1st The Queen's Dragoon Guards Regimental Museum, occupies another part of Cardiff Castle. (0222 222 253). 1st King's Dragoon Guards and the Queen's Bays (2nd Dragoon Guards). Fine collection of medals.

Northern Ireland:

ARMAGH. Regimental Museum The Royal Irish Fusiliers, Sovereign's House, The Mall, BT61 9AJ. (0861 522911). Includes the Armagh, Cavan and Managhan Militia units.

BELFAST. The Royal Ulster Rifles, Regimental H.Q., 5 Waring Street, BT1 2EW. (0232 232 086). Fine displays. (BAO).

ENNISKILLEN. Regimental Museum The Royal Inniskilling Fusiliers, The Castle, County Fermanagh. (0365 323 142).

AUCTIONEERS:

The following auction houses hold regular medal sales.

Bonhams, Montpelier Street, Knightsbridge, London SW7 1HH. (071 584 9161).

Buckland, Dix & Wood, No.1 Old Bond Street, London WC1X 3TD. (071 499 5022).

Glendining's, 101 New Bond Street, London W1Y 9LG. (071 493 2445).

Sotheby's, Medal Dept., Summers Place, Billingshurst, West Sussex RH14 9AD. (0403 783933).

Spink & Son Ltd., (who are also dealers) 5-7 King Street, St. James's, London SW1Y 6QS. (071 930 7888).

MEDAL DEALERS:

Baldwin, A.H. & sons Ltd., 11 Adelphi Terrace, London WC2N 6BJ. (071 839 1310).

Bostock Militaria, 15 Waller Close, Leek Wootton, near Warwick CV35 7QG. (0926 56381).

Boulden, Paul, 17 The Parade, The Barbican, Plymouth, Devon. (0752 221443).

Burman, P.A., Blackborough End, Middleton, Norfolk PE32 1SE. (0553 840350).

Carter, Mark, PO Box 470, Slough SL3 6RR. (0753 534777).

Clark, B. & L., 16 Lothian Road, Middlesborough, Cleveland TS4 2HR. (0642 240827).

Collet, N.W., PO Box 235, London SE23 1NS. (081 291 1435).

D.M.D., 6 Beehive Way, Reigate, Surrey RH2 8DY. (0737 240080).

Dixon, C.J. & A.J. Ltd., 23 Prospect Street, Bridlington, East Yorkshire YO15 2AE. (0262 676877).

Dunelme Coins & Medals, 7 Durham Road, Esh Winning, Durham DH7 9NW. (091 373 4446).

Dyas, M.J. & S.J., 30 Shaftmoor Lane, Acocks Green, Birmingham B27 7RS. (021 707 2808).

Gordons, Stand G12–13, Antique Market, 1–7 Davies Mews, London W1 1AR. (071 629 2851).

Great War Medals, 22 Selborne Road, London N14 7DH. (081 886 4120).

Hamilton, A.D. & Co., 7 St. Vincent Place, Glasgow G12 DW. (041 221 5423).

Holdich, Raymond D., 7 Whitcomb Street, London WC2 (071 930 1979).

Liverpool Medal Co. Ltd., 42 Bury Business Centre, Kay Street, Bury, Lancs BL9 6BU. (061 763 4610).

March Medals, 113 Gravelley Hill North, Erdington, Birmingham B23 6BJ. (021 384 4901).

Military Shop, 1350 Stratford Road, Hall Green, Birmingham B28 9EH. (021 778 4819).

Neate Militaria, PO Box 26, Newmarket,

Sufolk CB8 9JE. (0638 660288).

Romsey Medals, 5 Bell Street, Romsey, Hampshire SO51 8GY. (0794 512069).

Sterling Coins and Medals, 2 Somerset Road, Boscombe, Bournemouth, Hampshire. (0202 423881).

Toad Hall Medals, Court Road, Newton Ferrers, near Plymouth, South Devon PL8 1DH. (0752 872672).

Walland, F.S., 17 Gyllyngdune Gardens, Seven Kings, Essex IG3 9HH. (081 590 4389).

The only market devoted solely to medals is the Britannia Medal Fair which is held five times a year at the Victory Services Club, 63–79 Seymour Street, London W.2. For dates contact Mrs Robinson (0207 71869) or Mr Walland (081 590 4389).

Among the many MEDAL DEALERS throughout the world are:

Bonus Eventus Phaleristic, Aartshertoginnestraat 27, 8400 Ostend, Belgium. (050 812158).

Conglomerate Coins and Medals, 206 Adelaide Street, Brisbane Queensland 4000, Australia. (07 2211217).

Ursual, Eugene G., PO Box 8096, Ottawa, Ontario, Canda K1G 3H6. (1-613-521-9691).

PUBLICATIONS:

Medal News, published ten times per annum by Token Publishing Ltd., 105 High Street, Honiton, Devon EX14 8PE. (0404 45414).

BIBLIOGRAPHY:

Blacker, Lt. Col.V., *Operations of the British Army in India*, London 1821.

Dorling, Capt. H. Taprell and Guille, L.F., *Ribbons and Medals*, London 1965.

Dupuy, R.E. & T.N., *The Encyclopedia of Military History*, London 1970.

Fortescue, Hon. J.W., *History of the British Army*, various volumes, London 1899 to 1930.

Gordon, Major L.L., *British Battles & Medals*, Aldershot 1979.

Gould, R.W. and Capt. Douglas-Morris, K.J., *The Army of India Medal Roll*, London 1974.

Gould, R.W., *Locations of British Cavalry, Infantry and Machine Gun Units 1914–1922*, London 1977.

Hall, D., *British Orders, Decorations and Medals*, St. Ives 1973.

H.M.S.O., *Casualties and Medical Statistics of the Great War*, London 1931.

H.M.S.O., *Statistics of the Military Effort of the British Empire 1914–1920*, London 1922.

Hocking, C., *Dictionary of Disasters at Sea during the Age of Steam 1824–1962*, London 1969.

Irwin, D. Hastings, *War Medals and Decorations*, 4th Edition, London 1910.

Jerrold, D., *The Royal Naval Division*, London 1923.

Jones, G., *The Battle of Waterloo*, London 1852.

Keown-Boyd, H., *The Sudan Campaign*, London 1986.

Long, W.H., *Medals of the British Navy and how they were won*, London 1895.

Lummis, W.M. and Wynn, K.G., *Honour the Light Brigade*, London 1973.

Middlebrook, M., *The First Day on the Somme*, London 1971.

ORDERS AND MEDALS RESEARCH SOCIETY, various journals and dates.

Poulsom, Major N.W., *A Catalogue of Campaign and Independence medals issued during the Twentieth Century to the British Army*, Newcastle 1969.

Purves, A.A., *Collecting Medals and Decorations*, London 1968.

Steward, W.A., *War Medals and their History*, London 1915.

Token Publishing Ltd., *The Medals Year Book*, Honiton 1993.

Wise, A., *A Guide to Military Museums*, Powys 1992.

PRICE GUIDE FOR 1994

Since the last price guide, prices for campaign medals have generally kept pace with inflation and without any of the 'boom and bust' cycles which have afflicted other collecting fields. This of course is good, both for the hobby and the collector, and a deterrent to speculators.

The cost of Victorian material is rising, albeit slowly, although some single medals and 'heavy' groups can be difficult to place. At the other end of the range there is a strong and continuing interest in the First World War, especially medals to casualties, but pricing is difficult in an area in which there are so many permutations. For example, £15 to £20 for a World War I trio bears no relation to the cost of a similar group with a story. Thus a trio to an infantry sergeant killed in action on the Western Front may be unsaleable at £50 whilst similar medals to a R.F.C. sergeant pilot (shot down and killed over the same trench and on the same day as the soldier) will find willing buyers at £300 or more. The unsolicited distinction of being a victim of Richthofen, 'The Red Baron', will push the price towards £1,000!

Prices for trios to First Day of the Somme casualties also vary a great deal; officers' medals fetch £250 to £1,000, according to regiment or rank, with the ordinary P.B.I. lagging in the £75 to £150 bracket. Naval casualties have never reached the rarefied heights gained by the other two Services, but a trio to a rating K.I.A. on one of the capital ships at Jutland will still make £120.

Gulf War medals, in common with all new awards, can be expected to fall in price as more examples reach the market. However, this medal with the bar '2 AUGUST 1990' will always be scarce and the cost is unlikely to drop more than 25% from the current asking price of £800. Similarly, the most recent bars to the Campaign Service medal are commanding high prices and the 'N IRAQ & S TURKEY' clasp is on offer at £625. By contrast, the Northern Ireland clasp on the same medal, has now been in issue for nearly a quarter of a century. As a result, regrettably, it is very common and priced accordingly. Nevertheless, although this bar to the REME might not find a buyer at £20, a similar medal to a guardsman will fetch £35.

Basic prices in the following guide are those for a medal to a British private in an infantry of the line regiment. As a working rule, add 50% for officers, 20% for cavalry and 50% for guards. These figures are cumulative: a medal priced at £100 to an infantryman would rise to £150 for an officer and £180 for a cavalry officer. This, of course, is still fairly arbitrary; obviously an award to the colonel commanding will attract a still higher premium than the similar medal to an ensign. Finally, and with apologies to all gunners, sappers, medics, drivers and technicians – past, present and future – deduct 15% for campaign medals to members of Corps.

(F) indicates the existence of dangerous forgeries, often genuine medals which have been renamed to participants in famous actions, such as the Charge of the Light Brigade or Isandhlwana. Additions to this group concern the General Service Medal (Army and R.A.F.) with the bar S.E. Asia 1945–46 or Bomb and Mine Clearance 1945–49. A number of unnamed medals, bearing either of these clasps, have been shipped in from India and Australia and then fraudulently named in the United Kingdom. As far as the Campaign Service Medal is concerned, common clasps such as Northern Ireland have been removed and replaced with forged Dhofar or Lebanon bars. A similar switch will probably be made in the near future with the Kuwait clasp.

(C) stands for counterfeit and means that some unscrupulous citizen has been striking or casting copies of medals and/or clasps with intent to deceive. A typical example is the Indian Medal 1895, named in appropriate script and carrying a Defence of Chitral bar, which appeared in 1984. Both medal and clasp are spurious. Intending buyers may well require verification or some proof of provenance (not providence) before parting with money for expensive medals and bars.

(CP) is an abbreviation for 'collector's price' and indicates that the medal or clasp is so scarce that the price is literally what the collector is prepared to pay (usually four figures). All prices are in pounds sterling.

1. £300. Add 25% for medals to the following: 1 Royal Dragoons, 2 and 3/1 Foot Guards and 1/41 and 1/92 Foot (all of whom lost heavily at Quatre Bras). Add 50% to 1, 2 and 6 Dragoons (charge of the Union Brigade at Waterloo); + 50% for 2 Light Battalion K.G.L., (original defenders of La Haye Sainte); + 50% the four light companies of 1 and 2 Foot Guards (Defence of Hougoumont). Deduct 25% for the 2/35, 1/54, 2/59 and 1/91 Foot (all in Colville's reserve division and not in action).

2. Prices below are for single clasp medals, which in some cases are worth more than two or three bar awards.

Egypt £250
Maida £300
Roleia £525
Vimiera £300
Sahagun £350
Benevente (CP)
Sahagun and Benevente £400
Corunna £250
Martinique £250
Talavera £250
Guadaloupe £250
Busaco £250
Barrosa £250
Fuentes D'Onor £250
Albuhera £300
Java £350
Ciudad Rodrigo £275
Badajoz £280 (Deduct 25% for the 3/ , 1/8 and 2/38 on reserve).
Salamanca £275
Fort Detroit £975
Chateaguay Farm £950
Vittoria £200
Pyrenees £225
St. Sebastian £250
Nivelle £200
Nive £200
Orthes £200
Toulouse £200
2 clasps £250
3 clasps £300
4 clasps £350
5 clasps £375
6 clasps £425
7 clasps £475
8 clasps £575
9 clasps £750
10 clasps £850
11 clasps £1000
12 clasps £1400
13 clasps (CP)
14 clasps (CP)

3. Over 230 different clasps were authorised for this medal and some of these bars are extremely scarce, while others have never even appeared on the market. Thus only the most important, and available, single bars are shown below. Multiple bar medals are usually (CP). Privately commissioned and unauthorised clasps are known to exist and a typical example is 'DARDENELLES' (when the British forced a passage into the Sea of Marmora in 1807) which can be seen in the medal room at the National Maritime Museum.

In addition to fleet and single ship engagements there were also 56 clasps for cutting-out operations by ship's boats crews; but in only two of these actions did the number of issued clasps reach three figures. These were '1ST NOV., BOAT SERVICE 1809' (118 clasps) and '14TH DECEMBER BOAT SERVICE

1814' (214). Thus virtually any Boat Service bar commands at least £650.
Fleet Actions:
1 June 1794 £475 and to the Army £950
14th March 1795 £550
23rd June 1795 £500
St. Vincent £450
Camperdown £450
Nile £550
12th October 1798 £625
Egypt £350
Copenhagen £675
Trafalgar £800
Martinique £275
Gut of Gibraltar 12th July 1801 £500
4th November 1805 £425
Curacao 1st Jan. 1807 £600
Basque Roads, 1809 £300
Guadaloupe £275
Java £275
St. Domingo £325
St. Sebastian £350
The Potomac, 17th Aug., 1814 £975
Algiers £300
Navarino £275
Syria £175
Other Actions, including frigates:
Mars, 21st April 1798 £725
Lion, 15th July 1798 £850
Acre, 30th May 1799 £650
London, 13th March 1806 £750
Curacoa, 1st Jan., 1807 £600
Nassau, 22nd March 1808 £800
Stately, 22nd March 1808 £800
Seahorse with Badere Zaffer £950
Lissa £450
Off Tamatave, 20th May 1811 £400
Victorious wh. Rivoli £675
Shannon wh. Chesapeake (CP)
4. For engraved naming, including those medals to native troops, deduct 50%. Add 50% to the price of the first clasp for each additional bar on medals with impressed naming.
Allighur £2750
Battle of Delhi £3000
Assye £2250
Asseerghur £2850
Laswarree £1500
Gawilghur £2750
Argaum £2750
Defence of Delhi (CP)
Battle of Deig £2750
Capture of Deig £2000
Nepaul £550
Kirkee (CP)
Poona £900
Kirkee and Poona £950 and Bombay Marine £900
Seetabuldee (CP)
Nagpore (CP)
Seetabuldee and Nagpore (CP)
Maheidpoor £650
Corygaum (CP)
Ava £350, R.N. £450
Bhurtpoor £450
5. Unnamed £140. Named and verified £275. Indian troops £160.
6. (C) Candahar £350. (C) Cabul £225. Ghuznee and Cabul £350. Candahar, Ghuznee and Cabul £300. Deduct £100 for unnamed medals and those named to Indian troops.
7. Mural crown obverse £400. Victoria Vindex reverse £650. Unnamed medals deduct £200 and £400 respectively. Indian recipients less £200 from both.
8. First issue, unnamed, £600. Second issue, named and verified £2500. Deduct 50% for awards to native troops.
9. Royal Navy and British Army £200. Indian and Bengal Marine £300. Indian infantry £100.
10. Meanee £500. Hyderabad £325. Meanee-Hyderabad £350. Unnamed medals £150. Any reverse to a native £180.
11. (C) Maharajpoor Star £300. Punniar Star £275. Either unnamed £150. Add £25 for original brass hook suspender; deduct £75 for stars to natives. The copies of these stars are excellent, and therefore dangerous.
12. Moodkee £125, add £75 for each extra clasp. Ferozeshuhur £125, add £50 for each extra clasp. Aliwal £125, add £50 for each extra clasp. Sobraon £120. (Four different reverses).
13. £175.
14. No bar £120. One bar (scarcer than two-bar medals) £250. Two bars £200. Verified to 24th Foot at Chilianwala £450.
15. (IT) indicates Indian troops (no British infantry involved).
Pegu £75 (RN £85)
Persia £75
North West Frontier £85
Umbeyla £110
Bhootan £95
Looshai (IT) £140
Perak £95 (RN £110)
Jowaki 1877–8 £75
Naga 1879–80 (IT) £140
Burma 1885–7 £50 (RN £75)
Sikkim 1888 £110
Hazara 1888 £70
Burma 1887–89 £85*
Chin Lushai 1889–90 £110*
Samana 1891 £85*
Hazara 1891 £95*
N.E. Frontier 1891 £110*
Hunza 1891 (IT) £180*
Burma 1889–92 £60*
Lushai 1889–92 £100*
(* Any one of these eight clasps in bronze, £50)
Chin Hills 1892–93 £400. Indian troops £180; bronze £180.
Kachin Hills 1892–93 £700. Indian troops, or bronze, £300.
Waziristan 1894–95 £95, bronze £200
16. The following basic prices are for medals with officially impressed naming. Unnamed medals deduct 50% and in the case of regimentally or privately impressed deduct 25%.
No bar £60
(C) Alma £120
(C) Inkermann £165
(C) Balaklava £150
(C) Sebastopol £80
Azoff £200 (RN)
Multiple bars (excluding Balaklava):
2 bars £100
3 bars £150
4 bars £300
The Balaklava clasp, either singly or with others to participants in the following actions: Charge of the Heavy Brigade £550; (F) Charge of the Light Brigade £1800; 93rd Foot (Thin Red Line) £375.
17. Impressed naming £200, engraved £80 and unnamed £60. Officially impressed medals to the Sappers and Miners £750.
18. No bar £60
Delhi £120
Relief of Lucknow £120
Lucknow £100

Central India £125
Defence of Lucknow, to an original defender £500
Defence of Lucknow, to first relief force £300
Multiples: excluding Defence of Lucknow.
2 Bars £175
3 Bars £450
4 Bars £1000
(Bengal Horse Artillery).
Naval Brigade:
no bar £200
Lucknow £300
Relief of Lucknow £300
2 bars (commoner than a single clasp medal) £325

19. For officially impressed medals; no bar £125, any single bar £175. Two bars £225 and three bars £300. Deduct 40% for engraved and 50% for unnamed medals. Medals known with (F) engraving.

20. *First War:*
Undated £130
1845–46 £200
1845–47 £260
1846–47 £350
1846 £500
1847 £400
1848 (CP)
Second War:
Undated £90
1860 £500
1860–61 £150
1860–63 (CP)
1860–64 £450
1860–65 £225
1860–66 £200
1861 (CP)
1861–63 (CP)
1861–64 £200
1861–65 (CP)
1861–66 £175
1862–66 (CP)
1863 £400
1863–64 £200
1863–65 £225
1863–66 £170
1864 £250
1864–65 £200
1964–66 £175
1865 £275
1865–66 £200
1866 £170
Some of these dates, on awards to the Royal Navy, are rare and command substantial premiums over the above prices. In contrast, the dates 1845–47 and 1846–47 are only known to the R.N.

21. (F) Fenian Raid 1866 £125. (F) Fenian Raid 1870 £150. Two bars, both Fenian Raids, £200. (F) Red River 1870 £800. Three clasp medals (CP) – only twenty issued. One of these, to a General, can be seen in the Royal Green Jackets Museum at Winchester.

22. R.N. £190; British army £160; Indian army £110. Naval Rocket Brigade £350. These prices are for examples in pristine condition. Quite often the neck of the suspender has been broken and repaired.

23. No bar £140; with bar Coomassie £200. Deduct 50% for medals to natives.

24. No bar £90.
1877 £1000
1877–78 £200
1877–8–9 £230
1878 £275
1878–79 £200
1879 £150
Deduct 20% for medals to colonials and volunteers. Add 50% for medals to the defenders (chiefly 1/24 Foot) of Rorke's Drift and the R.N. Medals to verified Isandhlwana casualties fetch £1250 plus. Beware (F) naming to both groups of casualties.

25. No bar £45
Ali Musjid £75
Peiwar Kotal £90
Charasia £105
Kabul £80
Ahmed Khel £75
Kandahar £90
2 bars £120
3 bars £150
4 bars £300
Medals to 66 Foot killed at Maiwand £600. Awards to 'E' Battery, B Brigade, R.A. £400. Deduct 25% for medals to Indian troops.

26. (C) British troops £90; Indian troops and unnamed £60.

27. (F) Transkei £280. Basutoland £175. Bechuanaland £150. Two clasp medals £300. Three bars £850.

28. No bar £45
Alexandria £55
Tel-eb-Kebir £55
El-Teb £90
Gemaizah £90
Toski £160
Toski + Gemaizah £250
Tamaii £100
El-Teb-Tamaii £80
Suakin 1884 £55
The Nile 1884–85 £55
Suakin 1885 £60
Abu Klea + The Nile £175
Kirbekan + The Nile 1884–85 £140
Tofrek + Suakin 1885 £120
(Abu Klea and Tofrek not issued as single clasps).
The following multiple clasp prices are based on the most common bars:
2 bars £75
3 bars £130
4 bars £265
5 bars £450
6 bars (CP)
Medals to Canadian boatmen and the New South Wales Artillery – £450.
Khedive's Stars: undated £45 (with Tokar clasp £100); 1882 £25; 1884 £35 and 1884–86 £35.

29. No bar £165 and with bar £300. These prices are for medals to Canadians; medals to the nine British officers on the Canadian staff command a heavy premium. Deduct 25% for unnamed awards. This is not a popular medal with collectors.

30. 1887–8 £145
Witu 1890 £190
1891–92 £140
1892 £130
Witu August 1893 £190
Liwondi 1893 £900*
Juba River 1893 £900*
Lake Nyassa 1893 £925*
(*Add £400 for medals to the Royal Navy)
1893–94 £165
Gambia 1894 £140
Benin River 1894 £120
Brass River 1895 £140
M'Wele 1895–96 (engraved on rim of medal) £70
1896–98 £165
Niger 1897 £825
Benin 1897 £140
Dawkita 1897 (CP)
1897–98 £120
1898 £200 to R.N. £600
Sierra Leone 1898–99 £115
1899 £240, to R.N. £350
1900 £225
Multiple bars (usually to native troops or police) (CP)
Not a widely collected medal.

31. (F) Mashonaland 1890 £800. (F) Matabeleland with

1893 reverse £240, but to a Shangani River casualty, £1250. Rhodesia with 1896 reverse £220. Mashonaland with 1897 reverse £300. Multiple clasp medals (CP).

32. Without bar £150; with bar £250. Bronze £650. Unpopular.

33. (C) Defence of Chitral 1895 £600; in bronze (CP). Relief of Chitral 1895 £45. These two bars together £95.

Punjab Frontier 1897–98 £35, and in bronze £75. Punjab Frontier 1897–98 + Tirah 1897–98 £60; bronze £50. (Tirah not awarded as a single clasp). (C)

Malakand 1897 £95. Verified to a defender of Chakdara Fort £200. Bronze £75.

Samana 1897 (not awarded as a single clasp) + Punjab Frontier 1897–98 £80. In bronze £60. Verified 36th Sikhs in defence of Fort Gulistan £200.

Waziristan 1901–02 (almost certain to be found on a Edward VII obverse, and to Indian troops) £100. In bronze £60.

Other than Malakand, Waziristan and defenders, deduct 25% for silver medals to Indian troops.

34. (C) Regimentally named (2nd West Yorks.) £150. Unnamed £100.

35. £85. To the 21st Lancers who charged at Omdurman, £375. Bronze and unnamed, £150.

36. The following prices are for named medals to Egyptian or Sudanese soldiers. For the Atbara and Khartoum bars on medals to British troops, double the prices shown.

No bar (silver) £45
To the Royal Navy, £120
No bar (bronze) £70
Firket £60
Hafir £65
Abu Hamed £70
Sudan 1897 £70
The Atbara £35
Khartoum £35
The Atbara + Khartoum £75
Gedaref £90
Sudan 1899 £90
Bahr-el-Ghaza 1900–02 £110
Jerok £95
Nyam-Nyam £100
Talodi £100
Katfia £100
Nyima £110

Note: multiple clasps on unnamed medals or medals to Sudanese troops are not uncommon.

37. No clasp £180. Lubwa's £250, usually found in conjunction with Uganda 1897–98 £450. Uganda 1897–98 £225. 1898 £200, and in bronze £400. Uganda 1899 £250.

38. Without bar (silver) £35
Without bar (bronze) £75
Cape Colony £30
(C) Natal £45
(C) Rhodesia £130
Relief of Mafeking £120
Defence of Kimberley £120
Talana £90
Elandslaagte £145
Defence of Ladysmith £50
Belmont £45
Modder River £45
(C) Relief of Kimberley £70
Paardeberg £40
Orange Free State £20
Relief of Ladysmith £40
Driefontein £40
Wepener £175
(C) Defence of Mafeking £450
Transvaal £25
Johannesburg £30
Laing's Nek £40
Diamond Hill £40
Wittebergen £35
Belfast £40
South Africa 1901 £10
South Africa 1902 £10

Multiple clasp medals:

2 bars (not including either dated clasps) £35.

3 bars £40. 4 bars £50. 5 bars £65. 6 bars £90. 7 bars £150. 8 bars (CP). Prices do not include the scarce clasps or the two dated bars. Some clasps are much rarer as singles, but may be common when grouped on a multi-bar medal.

Reverse with dates in relief (not 'ghost' dates) £850.

Add 50% to any clasp on medals to the R.N. or Royal Marines.

39. Not awarded without a clasp, except to nursing sisters, and very rarely authorised with only one bar. Two bars £20 to the Army but (CP) on medals to the Royal Navy. One bar (documented verification essential) £200.

40. £100 to £125 according to regiment.

41. South Africa 1899–1902 £250. China 1900 £350. Both bars £475.

42. No bar, silver, £60. Taku Forts, only to the R.N., £185. Defence of Legations (CP). Two bars (excluding Defence of Legations) £275. Bronze, no bar, £90 and Relief of Pekin £150.

43. Without bar £125, bronze £225. With clasp Kumassi £200 and in bronze, £400. Not a popular medal.

44. No bar, in bronze, £110
N. Nigeria £130
N. Nigeria 1902 £120
N. Nigeria 1903 £110
N. Nigeria 1903–4 £150
N. Nigeria 1904 £140
N. Nigeria 1906 £150
S. Nigeria £225
S. Nigeria 1902 £160
S. Nigeria 1902–03 £160
S. Nigeria 1903 £155
S. Nigeria 1903–04 £175
S. Nigeria 1904 £160
S. Nigeria 1904–05 £175
S. Nigeria 1905 £250
S. Nigeria 1905–06 £160
Uganda 1900 £200
East Africa 1902 £300
East AFrica 1904 £200
East Africa 1905 £175
East Africa 1906 £160
West Africa 1906 £160
West Africa 1908 £190
West Africa 1909–10 £180
Somaliland 1901 £240
Somaliland 1902–1904*(I) plus Jidballi (I) (latter not awarded as a single clasp) £135
Somaliland 1908–10* £70
B.C.A. 1899–1900 £220
Jubaland*(I) £165
Gambia* £140
Arc 1901–1902 £150
Lango 1901 £250
Kissi 1905 £275
Nandi 1905–06 £275
Shimber Berris 1914–15 (I) £200
Nyasaland 1915 £225
East Africa 1913 £225
East Africa 1914 £200
East Africa 1913–14 £175
Jubaland 1917–18 £180
East Africa 1918 £175
Nigeria 1918 £165

Somaliland 1920*(I)
£140.R.A.F. £250
Kenya £40
Bronze medals and clasps:
Jubaland £200
Somaliland 1901 £180
Somaliland 1902–04 £55
Somaliland 1908–10* £80
(*These clasps were also awarded to the Royal Navy. (I) These bars were earned by Indian troops, in addition to Africans.)
With the exception of clasps to the Royal Navy, Indian troops or the bar 'Kenya', most of these medals were awarded to African soldiers and policemen. Medals to British officers and N.C.O.s carry a substantial premium.
45. Without bar £125; with clasp (C) Gyantse £300. Bronze no bar £45, with bar £125. Deduct 50% for silver medals to native troops.
46. No bar £90, with bar £125. Although much scarcer without a bar such a medal is not so popular with collectors. Add 25% for awards to colonial volunteers.
47. North West Frontier 1908 £50, in bronze £45. Abor 1911–12, to a British officer £275. Indian recipient £125. Bronze £175.
Afghanistan N.W.F. 1919, £30. R.A.F. £100
Waziristan 1919–21 £30.
Mahsud 1919–20, extremely rare as a single clasp (CP) and usually found in conjunction with the previous bar.
Both bars £60; R.A.F. £120.
Malabar 1921–22 £75
Waziristan 1921–24 £35. R.A.F. £75
Waziristan 1925 (only awarded to R.A.F. personnel) £375.
North West Frontier 1930–31 £45. R.A.F. £80.
Burma 1930–32 £45. R.A.F. £500.
Mohmand 1933. Indian troops £35. British (artillery or armoured car) £125. R.A.F. £250.
North West Frontier 1935 £40. R.A.F. £75.
Unless separately indicated, these prices are for medals to British troops. Indian units deduct 50%.
48. Prices based on unnamed medals, as issued. No bar, silver, £80. Bronze, not issued with a bar, £140. Add £180 for each clasp.
49. With original clasp £20. Large numbers of reproduction clasps, in many different styles, have appeared over the past seventy years.
50. £3. (F). Genuine stars have been fraudulently renamed.
51. £6; bronze £35.
ITEMS ***49/50/51/53:*** *see remarks in preamble to price guide regarding wide variations in the pricing of World War I trios.*
52. £8.
53. £1. South African issue £10.
54. £35.
55. Persian Gulf 1909–14 £65.
Iraq 1919–20 £650.
N.W. Persia 1920 (CP)
Palestine 1936–39 £55.
S.E. Asia 1945–46 £110.
Minesweeping 1945–51 £80.
Palestine 1945–48 £45.
Malaya £60.
Yangtze 1949 (to H.M.S. *Amethyst*) £450. Other ships £250.
Bomb and Mine Clearance 1945–53 £400.
Bomb and Mine Clearance Mediterranean £650.
Cyprus £50.
Near East £55.
Arabian Peninsula £85.
Brunei £120.
56. S. Persia. British officers £95; other ranks (mostly specialists) £150. R.A.F. £425.
Indian troops £40.
Kurdistan. £55, R.A.F. £250.
Iraq.£40, R.A.F. £175.
N.W. Persia. £60. R.A.F. £250.
Southern Desert, Iraq (only awarded to RAF personnel) £250.
Northern Kurdistan. R.A.F. £350. Iraq Levies £100.
Palestine £30.
(F) S.E. Asia 1945–46. £50.
(F) Bomb and Mine Clearance 1945–49. £225.
Palestine 1945–48. £25.
Malaya. £25.
Cyprus. £20.
Near East. £45.
Arabian Peninsula. £45.
Brunei. £100.
Unless otherwise shown, these prices are for medals to British troops. Indian and local units deduct 50%.
57. One clasp £45, R.A.F. £65. Both bars £60 and to the R.A.F. £85. Indian units deduct 50%.
Note: 58 to 65 have all been (C). Prices of stars with a clasp, especially the Battle of Britain bar, are for those with documented verification.
58. £4. With Battle of Britain clasp, £150.
59. £12. Air Crew Europe bar, £75. France and Germany bar, £20.
60. £90. With Atlantic or France and Germany clasp, £110.
61. £5. 8th or 1st Army clasp, £10. North Africa bar, £15.
62. £20. With bar Burma; R.N. £35, army personnel, £50.
63. £10. Pacific clasp, £15.
64. £5.
65. £12. With Atlantic bar, £25.
66. £6.
67. £3.
68. R.N. £45; R.A.F. £65 and Army £55; but Gloucestershire Regiment, Royal Ulster Rifles and Duke of Wellington's respectively £175, £85 and £100.
69. Borneo £30
Radfan £45.
South Vietnam (CP)
South Arabia £30
Malay Peninsula £35
Northern Ireland £20/35
Dhofar £150
Lebanon £600
Mine Clearance:
Gulf of Suez £325.
Gulf £425.
Kuwait £800.
N. Iraq & Sth Turkey £625.
70. £85. Note: certain medals awarded to Australians have reached the U.K. market in peculiar circumstances.
71. With rosette, £180, without rosette £140. Auxiliaries and merchant ships £120. 2nd Bn. The Parachute Regiment (Battle of Goose Green) £275.
72. No clasp, £100. 16 Jan–28 Feb 1991 bar, £150. 2 Aug 1990 bar, £800.

1. Waterloo Medal. 18th June 1815

The Battle of Waterloo, which changed the course of history and gave employment to numerous authors, publishers and cameramen, was also responsible for a silver medal–a medal with three distinctions. It was the first medal to be awarded by the British Crown to all its troops irrespective of rank, the first campaign medal to be given to the next-of-kin of men killed in action and the first medal to have the recipient's name impressed by a machine. Although named the Waterloo medal it was actually awarded, at the suggestion of the Duke of Wellington, for Quatre Bras on the 16th, the fighting on the 17th and Waterloo proper on the 18th. Every British and King's German Legion soldier present at these actions was credited with two years' extra service to count for pay, promotion and pension.

This medal, 1.4in in diameter, was instituted by an order dated 10th March 1816 and a later instruction was issued that the ribbon was never to be worn without the medal. The Waterloo veterans, justly proud of their award, promptly wore the medal in all weathers and, if contemporary accounts are true, many of the discharged rank and file often wore it with civilian clothes. As a result, the steel ring through which the ribbon was threaded often rusted and many recipients replaced the ring with some form of silver suspension of their own design. For the Peninsular veterans these suspenders were sometimes engraved, or carried unofficial clasps, bearing the names of previous battles and actions. Since the ribbon was normally sewn on the jacket some officers provided themselves with duplicates (one for each uniform) which were usually other ranks' medals with the original recipient's particulars erased. A copy of the Waterloo medal also made an appearance, slightly smaller and thinner than the official award and omitting the designer's name. This was possibly made for a similar reason or, as depicted in prints of the period, to allow a wife to wear a replica of her husband's medal on gala occasions.

On the obverse of the medal, designed by T. Wyon, is the laureated head of the Prince Regent and the legend GEORGE P. REGENT. The nicely balanced reverse depicts the Grecian winged figure of Victory, seated on a pedestal, holding a palm branch in her right hand and an olive branch in her left. Above her head is the word WELLINGTON and in a rectangle, below the pedestal, the word WATERLOO. Beneath the rectangle is the date JUNE 18 1815 in two lines. The ribbon is crimson with quarter-inch wide dark blue edges. The individual naming is in large impressed capitals and always includes the regiment or unit; the blank spaces at either end are usually filled by two or three stars. Suspension is by means of a steel clip, sweated to the top of the medal, through which passed a steel ring 1.1in in diameter.

2. Military General Service Medal 1793–1814

A medal for twenty-one years war service, but with bars which cover only thirteen of those years; authorised forty-six years after the first campaign it commemorates; issued fifty-five years after the first date on the medal and then only to survivors and, finally, bearing the head of a sovereign not even born when some of the earlier engagements were fought–such is the 'Dead Man's Medal'. Although the survivors of 1815 proudly wore their Waterloo medals, the veterans of the other battles of the Napoleonic Wars had nothing to show for their services, except scars, despite efforts made on their behalf by the Duke of Richmond. However, not until a medal for the Scinde Wars of 1843 was granted by the British Government did mounting public opinion overcome the opposition of the Duke of Wellington (and probably the Exchequer). A silver medal was finally instituted in 1847, together with twenty-eight clasps covering actions between 1806 and 1814; then in 1850 a further Order authorised a clasp for Egypt, 1801.

The twenty-nine bars finally authorised were as follows:
EGYPT (2nd March to 2nd September 1801) MAIDA (4th July 1806) ROLEIA (17th August 1808) VIMIERA (21st August 1808) SAHAGUN (21st December 1808) BENEVENTE (29th December 1808) SAHAGUN AND BENEVENTE (Awarded to those present at both actions) CORUNNA (16th January 1809) MARTINIQUE (30th January to 24th February 1809) TALAVERA (27th and 28th July 1809) GUADALOUPE (January and February 1810) BUSACO (27th September 1810) BARROSA (5th March 1811) FUENTES D'ONOR (5th May 1811) ALBUHERA (16th May 1811) JAVA (10th to 26th August 1811) CIUDAD RODRIGO (8th to 19th January 1812) BADAJOZ (17th March to 6th April 1812) SALAMANCA (22nd July 1812) FORT DETROIT (August 1812) VITTORIA (21st June 1813) PYRENEES (25th July to 2nd August 1813) ST. SEBASTIAN (17th July to 8th September 1813) CHATEAUGUAY (26th October 1813) NIVELLE (10th November 1813) CHRYSTLER'S FARM (11th November 1813) NIVE (9th to 13th December 1813) ORTHES (27th Feburary 1814) TOULOUSE (10th April 1814).

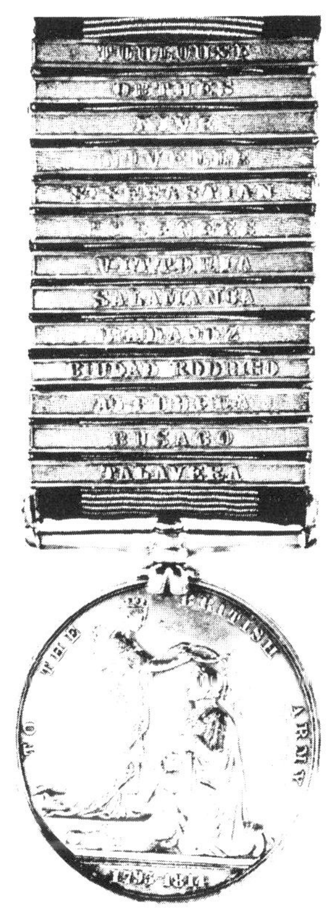

The first date on the medal seems to indicate that clasps for earlier actions were contemplated, possibly Lincelles or Nieuport in Flanders, in August and October 1793 respectively. In any case, there are some surprising omissions from the final lists of clasps, namely the capture of the Cape of Good Hope from the Dutch in 1806 with the loss of only 16 killed and 137 wounded and the brilliant victory at Kioge, outside Copenhagen, in the following year. Prisoners, guns, stores, sixty-four ships of the Danish Fleet, the Island of Heligoland and nearly £1,000,000 in prize money–all this for total British casualties of 43 killed and 145 wounded. The cavalry action at Sahagun (2 killed and 18 wounded) earned a clasp; but not so Wellington's first victory in the Peninsula, the passage of the Douro where there were 119 casualties. The capture of Guadaloupe in 1810 (273 casualties) merited a bar, but not the taking of St. Lucia in 1796 with 405 men dead and wounded. Similar examples could be repeated indefinitely, but it is strange that all these engagements won battle honours for the units engaged, but not battle clasps. Nearly 26,000 medals were issued, a surprising number considering the passage of time, bearing between them about 84,000 clasps. The number of clasps per medal ranged from fifteen awarded to two recipients, to over eight thousand with only one. Whilst the double figure clasps are most impressive, some of the medals with fewer bars show an amazing range of service and years. Richard Wittle's ten years with the 90th Foot, for example, only earned him three clasps but he ranged as far afield as Egypt, Martinique and Guadaloupe.

On the obverse of the medal is the diademed head of Queen Victoria with the legend VICTORIA REGINA and the date 1848. The reverse shows the young Queen standing on a dais about to place a laurel wreath on the head of the Duke of Wellington, who is kneeling before her and holding his Field Marshal's Baton. Beside the dais is a small British Lion dormant and in the exergue below are the dates 1793-1814. Following the curve of the upper half circle of the medal is the inscription TO THE BRITISH ARMY. It was designed by W. Wyon and the ribbon is crimson with eight-of-an-inch wide dark blue borders. The individual naming is in large, impressed capitals and the rank, name and unit is always shown. The medal was never issued without a bar.

3. Naval General Service Medal 1793–1840

In common with the victories of their military brethren, the brilliant successes of the officers and men of the Royal Navy during the Napoleonic Wars went unrecognized until a General Order dated 1st June 1847 authorised the striking of a medal to cover the years 1793 to 1815. A later Order extended the qualifying dates to include the fleet actions at Algiers in 1816, Navarino in 1827 and the coast of Syria in 1840. A total of 231 were authorised which not only covered famous battles such as Camperdown, Nile, Trafalgar, and so on, but also a large number of single ship and cutting-out actions. However, after a lapse of so many years, it is perhaps not surprising that only about 21,000 medals were actually claimed and there were no claimants for several of the bars. The medal was never issued without a bar and a total of about 24,000 bars were awarded; but nearly 10,000 of these commemorated the three later battles fought between 1816 and 1840.

The maximum number of bars issued with any one medal was seven and there were two such medals, both to officers. In common with other campaign medals only the recipients knew the true worth of the award. During the battle of the Glorious First of June, a son was born to a Mrs. McKenzie on board H.M.S. TREMENDOUS; fifty-four years later Daniel Tremendous McKenzie duly received his medal with the bar 1ST JUNE 1794, awarded for a battle on the day he was born. The fourteen claimants who had served on H.M.S. AGINCOURT, a 64gun ship of the line, no doubt received their medals with pride, despite the fact that their captain was court-martialled after the battle for failing to bring his ship into close action. On the other hand, it appears that many of the veterans did not receive the full tally of bars to which they were entitled.

In the following list of bars, the dates in brackets for fleet and ship actions are given for reference–the dates do not appear on the actual clasps. The abbreviation WH on bars indicates 'with' and BOAT SERVICE commemorates numerous 'cutting-out' and similar engagements by crews of ships' boats.

15 MARCH BOAT SERVICE 1793
NYMPHE 18th JUNE 1793
CRESCENT 20 OCTR. 1793
ZEBRA 17 MARCH 1794
17 MAR. BOAT SERVICE 1794
CARYSFORT 29 MAY 1794
1 JUNE 1794
ROMNEY 17 JUNE 1794
BLANCHE 4 JANY. 1795
LIVELY 13 MARCH 1795
14 MARCH 1795
ASTRAEA 10 APRIL 1795
THETIS 17 MAY 1795
HUSSAR 17 MAY 1795

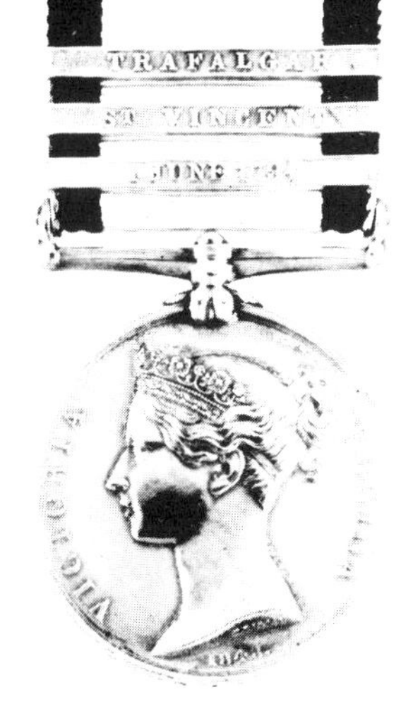

MOSQUITO 9 JUNE 1795
17 JUNE 1795
23rd JUNE 1795
DIDO 24 JUNE 1795
LOWESTOFFE 24 JUNE 1795
SPIDER 25 AUGT. 1795
PORT SPERGUI (17 March 1796)
INDEFATIGABLE 20 APL. 1796
UNICORN 8 JUNE 1796
STA. MARGARITTA 8 JUNE 1796
SOUTHAMPTON 9 JUNE 1796
DRYAD 13 JUNE 1796
TERPSICHORE 13 OCTR. 1796
LAPWING 3 DECR. 1796
MINERVE 19 DECR. 1796
BLANCHE 19 DEC. 1796
INDEFATIGABLE 13 JANY. 1797
AMAZON 13 JANY. 1797
ST. VINCENT (14th February 1797)
SAN FIORENZO 8 MARCH 1797
NYMPHE 8 MARCH 1797
29 MAY BOAT SERVICE 1797
CAMPERDOWN (11th October 1797)
PHOEBE 21 DECR. 1797
MARS 21 APRIL 1798
ISLE ST. MARCOU (6 May 1798)
LION 15 JULY 1798
NILE (1st August 1798)
ESPOIR 7 AUGT. 1798
12th OCTOBER 1798
FISGARD 20 OCTR. 1798
SYBILLE 28 FEBY. 1799
TELEGRAPH 18 MARCH 1799
ACRE (20 May 1799)
9 JUNE BOAT SERVICE 1799
SCHIERMONNIKOOG 12 AUGT. 1799
ARROW 13 SEPT. 1799
WOLVERINE 13 SEPT. 1799
SURPRISE WITH HERMIONE (25th October 1799)
SPEEDY 6 NOVR. 1799
COURIER 23 NOVR. 1799
20 DEC. BOAT SERVICE 1799
VIPER 26 DECR. 1799
FAIRY 5 FEB. 1800
HARPY 5 FEBY. 1800
PETEREL 21 MARCH 1800
PENELOPE 30 MARCH 1800
VINCIEGO 30 MARCH 1800
CAPTURE OF THE DESIREE (8th July 1800)
29 JULY BOAT SERVICE 1800
SEINE 20 AUGT. 1800
29 AUG. BOAT SERVICE 1800
27 OCT. BOAT SERVICE 1800
PHOEBE 19 FEBY. 1801
EGYPT (March-September 1801)
COPENHAGEN 1801 (2 April 1801)
SPEEDY 6 MAY 1801
GUT OF GIBRALTAR 12 JULY 1801
21 JULY BOAT SERVICE 1801
SYLPH 28 SEPTR. 1801
PASLEY 28 OCTR. 1801
27 JUNE BOAT SERVICE 1803
4 NOV. BOAT SERVICE 1803
4 FEB. BOAT SERVICE 1804
SCORPION 31 MARCH 1804
BEAVER 31 MARCH 1804
CENTURION 18 SEPT. 1804
ARROW 3 FEBY. 1805

ACHERON 3 FEBY. 1805
SAN FIORENZO 14 FEBY. 1805
4 JUNE BOAT SERVICE 1805
PHOENIX 10 AUGT. 1805
TRAFALGAR (21st October 1805)
4 NOVR. 1805
ST. DOMINGO (6th February 1806)
LONDON 13 MARCH 1806
AMAZON 13 MARCH 1806
PIQUE 26 MARCH 1806
SIRIUS 17 APRIL 1806
16 JULY BOAT SERVICE 1806
BLANCHE 19 JULY 1806
ARETHUSA 23 AUGT. 1806
ANSON 23 AUGT. 1806
CURACOA 1 JANY. 1807
2 JAN. BOAT SERVICE 1807
PICKLE 3 JANY. 1807
21 JAN. BOAT SERVICE 1807
19 APL. BOAT SERVICE 1807
HYDRA 6 AUGT. 1807
COMUS 15 AUGT. 1807
LOUISA 28 OCTR. 1807
CARRIER 14 NOVR. 1807
ANN 24 NOVR. 1807
13 FEB. BOAT SERVICE 1808
SAPPHO 2 MARCH 1808
SAN FIORENZO 8 MARCH 1808
EMERALD 13 MARCH 1808
CHILDERS 14 MARCH 1808
STATELY 22 MARCH 1808
NASSAU 22 MARCH 1808
OFF ROTA 4 APRIL 1808
GRASSHOPPER 24 APRIL 1808
RAPID 24 APRIL 1808
REDWING 7 MAY 1808
VIRGINIE 19 MAY 1808
REDWING 31 MAY 1808
SEAHORSE WH. BADERE ZAFFER (6th July 1808)
10 JULY BOAT SERVICE 1808
COMET 11 AUGT. 1808
11 AUG. BOAT SERVICE 1808
CENTAUR 26 AUGT. 1808
IMPLACABLE 26 AUGT. 1808
CRUIZER 1 NOVR. 1808
AMETHYST WH. THETIS (10th November 1808)
28 NOV. BOAT SERVICE 1808
OFF THE PEARL ROCK 13 DECR. 1808
ONYX 1 JANY. 1809
CONFIANCE 14 JANY. 1809
MARTINIQUE (February 1809)
HORATIO 10 FEBY. 1809
SUPERIEURE 10 FEBY. 1809
AMETHYST 5 APRIL 1809
BASQUE ROADS 1809 (12th April)
POMPEE 17 JUNE 1809
CASTOR 17 JUNE 1809
RECRUIT 17 JUNE 1809
CYANE 25-27 JUNE 1809
L'ESPOIR 25-27 JUNE 1809
BONNE CITOYENNE WH. FURIEUSE (6th July 1809)
7 JULY BOAT SERVICE 1809
14 JULY BOAT SERVICE 1809
25 JULY BOAT SERVICE 1809
27 JULY BOAT SERVICE 1809
29 JULY BOAT SERVICE 1809
28 AUG. BOAT SERVICE 1809
DIANA 11 SEPT. 1809
1 NOV. BOAT SERVICE 1809
13 DEC. BOAT SERVICE 1809
ANSE LA BARQUE 18 DECR. 1809
CHEROKEE 10 JANY. 1810
SCORPION 12 JANY. 1810
GUADALOUPE (January-February 1810)
THISTLE 10 FEBY. 1810
13 FEB. BOAT SERVICE 1810
SURLY 24 APRIL 1810
FIRM 24 APRIL 1810
SYLVIA 26 APRIL 1810
1 MAY BOAT SERVICE 1810
SPARTAN 3 MAY 1810
ROYALIST MAY & JUNE 1810
28 JUNE BOAT SERVICE 1810
AMANTHEA 25 JULY 1810
BANDA NEIRA (9th August 1810)
BOADICEA 18 SEPT. 1810
OTTER 18 SEPT. 1810
STAUNCH 18 SEPT. 1810
27 SEPT. BOAT SERVICE 1810
BRISEIS 14 OCTR. 1810
4 NOV. BOAT SERVICE 1810
23 NOV. BOAT SERVICE 1810
24 DEC. BOAT SERVICE 1810
LISSA (13th March 1811)
ANHOLT 27 MARCH 1811
ARROW 6 APRIL 1811
4 MAY BOAT SERVICE 1811
OFF TAMATAVE 20 MAY 1811
30 JULY BOAT SERVICE 1811
2 AUG. BOAT SERVICE 1811
HAWKE 18 AUGT. 1811
JAVA (August-September 1811)
20 SEPT. BOAT SERVICE 1811
SKYLARK 11 NOVR. 1811
LOCUST 11 NOVR. 1811
PELAGOSA 29 NOVR. 1811
4 DEC. BOAT SERVICE 1811
VICTORIOUS WH. RIVOLI (22nd February 1812)
WEASEL 22 FEBY. 1812
ROSARIO 27 MARCH 1812
GRIFFON 27 MARCH 1812
4 APL. BOAT SERVICE 1812
NORTHUMBERLAND 22 MAY 1812
GROWLER 22 MAY 1812
MALAGA 29 MAY 1812
OFF MARDOE 6 JULY 1812
SEALARK 21 JULY 1812
1 SEPT. BOAT SERVICE 1812
17 SEPT. BOAT SERVICE 1812
29 SEPT. BOAT SERVICE 1812
ROYALIST 29 DECR. 1812
6 JANY. BOAT SERVICE 1813
21 MARCH BOAT SERVICE 1813
WEASEL 22 APRIL 1813
28 APRIL BOAT SERVICE 1813
APL. & MAY BOAT SERVICE 1813
2 MAY BOAT SERVICE 1813

SHANNON WH. CHESAPEAKE (1st June 1813)
PELICAN 14 AUGT. 1813
ST. SEBASTIAN (August-September 1813)
THUNDER 9 OCTR. 1813
GLUCKSTADT 5 JANY. 1814
VENERABLE 16 JANY. 1814
CYANE 16 JANY. 1814
EUROTAS 25 FEBY. 1814
HEBRUS WH. L'ETOILE (27th March 1814)
PHOEBE 28 MARCH 1814
CHERUB 28 MARCH 1814
8 APL. BOAT SERVICE 1814
24 MAY BOAT SERVICE 1814
THE POTOMAC 17 AUGT. 1814
3 & 6 SEPT. BOAT SERVICE 1814
14 DEC. BOAT SERVICE 1814
ENDYMION WH. PRESIDENT (15th January 1815)
PILOT 17 JUNE 1815
GAIETA 24 JULY 1815
ALGIERS (27th August 1816)
NAVARINO (20th October 1827)
SYRIA (November 1840)

The obverse of the medal is similar to the Military General Service medal. The reverse shows the figure of Britannia holding a trident and seated on a seahorse. It was designed by W. Wyon and the ribbon is white with blue edges. The individual naming is indented in Roman capitals and the rank is only included if the recipient is an officer or warrant officer; the name of the ship is never given.

4. Army of India 1799–1826

The London Gazette of 28th February 1851 carried an official notice that the Honourable East India Company had been authorised to issue a medal to all survivors of the forces who had seen active service in India between 1799 and 1826. However, active service and disease in India, coupled with the passage of time, had left few claimants for the award. Over 40,000 men had fought in the six general actions of the First Mahratta War, for which clasps were awarded, but less than two hundred lived to claim their medals. The 1st Bengal European Regiment (later the Royal Munster Fusiliers) was over eight hundred strong the evening before the Battle of Deig, but only three of them were still alive to claim their medals in 1851. The clasp for Bhurtpore commemorated the successful attack in 1826; there was no award for the four unsuccessful attempts to storm the city in 1803, which cost over 3,000 casualties, (killed and wounded). Bhurtpore incidentally was seven miles in circumference with high mud walls, sixty feet thick, garrisoned by 20,000 men and reckoned to be impregnable. At 8 o'clock on the morning of 18th January 1826 a mine containing 10,000 pounds of black powder was exploded under one of the walls. Amid still-falling debris and clouds of dust, the storming columns surged forward into the breach, the forlorn hope carrying a black flag to show that no quarter would be given. Such was the type of savage fighting commemorated by this medal.

Twenty-one clasps were finally authorised, as shown below, and the medal was never issued without a clasp, or unnamed. The order of the bars is different to most awards in that the last clasp is nearest the medal (in other words the correct order reads downwards).

ALLIGHUR (4th September 1803)
Storming of Fort Allighur in the First Mahratta War.

BATTLE OF DELHI (11th September 1803) Scinde Army of 20,000 defeated by Lord Lake.

ASSAYE (23rd September 1803) The first of Wellington's victories with 4,000 troops against a French officered native army of 50,000.

ASSEERGHUR (21st October 1803) Surrender of Fort Asseerghur.
LASWARREE (1st November 1803) The Mahratta Army marching to recapture Delhi, defeated and dispersed with heavy casualties.
ARGAUM (29th November 1803) Battle on the plain of Argaum.
GAWILGHUR (15th December 1803) Siege and assault of a fortress of that name.
DEFENCE OF DELHI (8th-14th October 1804) Attempt by Holkar to recapture the city.
BATTLE OF DEIG (13th November 1804) A heavily contested battle near River Jumna.
CAPTURE OF DEIG (11th-23rd December 1804) Siege and storming of the fortress.
NEPAUL (October 1814-March 1816) A two year campaign against the Gurkhas.
KIRKEE (5th November 1817) A Mahratta army of 26,000 defeated near Poona.
POONA (11th-16th November 1817) The taking of Poona.
KIRKEE AND POONA. Awarded to troops engaged in both actions.
SEETABULDEE (26th-27th November 1817) The defeat of the army of the Rajah of Berar, near the city of Nagpore. Although sanctioned, it is doubtful whether this clasp was ever actually claimed.
NAGPORE (16th December 1817) Siege and surrender of the city of Nagpore.
SEETABULDEE AND NAGPORE. Awarded to troops engaged in both actions.
MAHEIDPOOR (21st December 1817) Battle against the Pindarries.
CORYGAUM (1st January 1818) British column successfully defended itself against attack by over 28,000 enemy cavalry and infantry.
AVA (1824-1826) Campaign in Burma– the only clasp for which the Royal Navy qualified.
BHURTPOOR (17th-18th January 1826) See text.

Drummer Colston of the 15th and 31st Native Infantry was the only recipient of a medal with seven clasps, and these covered a period of twenty-three years continuous service in India, from Allighur in 1803 to Bhurtpore in 1826. The medal rolls also record that just over three hundred men held the Army of India medal in conjunction with the Military General Service medal, and of these twenty-three also received the Waterloo medal.

On the reverse of the medal is the seated figure of Victory holding a laurel branch in her right hand and a wreath in her left. Against a palm tree in the left background is a trophy of arms, consisting of Indian armour and weapons. The inscription TO THE ARMY OF INDIA follows the curve of the upper half circle of the medal, while in the exergue below are the dates 1799-1826. The obverse, similar to plate 2, shows the diademed head of Queen Victoria with the legend VICTORIA REGINA. An ornate swivelling suspender, the prototype for many mid-Victorian campaign medals, holds the light blue ribbon. Naming is usually in large impressed capitals to British regiments and engraved in running script to Indian troops.

5. Ghuznee Medal 21st–23rd July 1839

The First Afghan War proved very prolific in honours and medals, and the storming of the fortress of Ghuznee appears to have set the pattern. This action earned the commander-in-chief a peerage, field officers and above the Order of the Dooranee Empire, all ranks were awarded the Ghuznee Medal and the eleven regiments concerned were each granted a battle honour–all this for less than 150 casualties, most of them wounded.

On the obverse of the medal is the fortress of Ghuznee with the name GHUZNEE below in a curved exergue. The reverse shows a mural crown with the date 23RD JULY above and the year 1839 below; the whole is surrounded by a laurel wreath, with a space for the recipient's name. The piece is 1.46in in diameter and the ribbon is 1.5in wide. The ribbon was originally half green, half yellow, but was changed to the present colour of half crimson and half green. Suspension is by means of a straight suspender and attachment, sweated onto the top of the medal. Apparently two separate dies were used for the obverse, as one type has a much wider border than the other. The awards were issued unnamed and consequently there is a wide variety in the styles of naming (privately executed) which may be found on the reverse or on the rim.

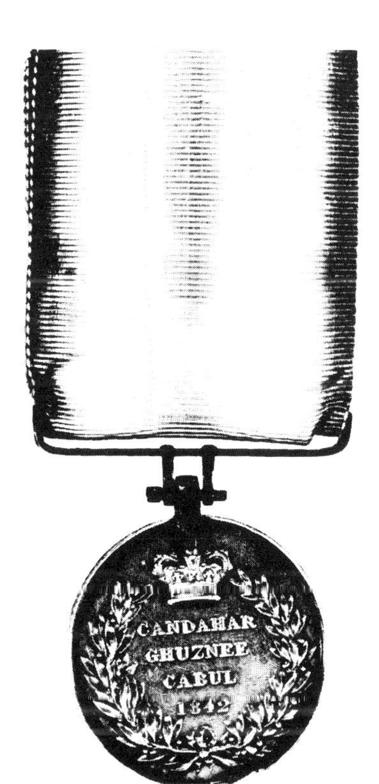

6. Candahar, Ghuznee and Cabul Medals October 1841 – October 1842. First Afghan War

There are four different strikings of this silver medal, which was authorised by a General Order in India in October 1842, but only one medal could be earned by any one man. This medal commemorates the somewhat confused fighting in North West India and Afghanistan with casualties which would have passed unnoticed in the wars of the twentieth century. General Nott's army for example, in the skirmish outside the fortress of Ghuznee in August 1842, had 24 killed–only two of whom were British–and earned battle honours for six regiments. It appears that the Indian Government was much more liberal with its honours than the Crown–no wonder the Peninsular veterans are reported to have been enraged.

The obverse of each medal is the same and bears the familiar diademed head of young Queen Victoria but with the legend VICTORIA VINDEX. The reverse side of each medal is as follows:

1. CANDAHAR with the date 1842 underneath, the whole surrounded by a laurel wreath and surmounted by a crown.
2. CABUL instead of CANDAHAR, otherwise similar.
3. Two entwined laurel wreaths, practically forming two circles, with GHUZNEE in the first loop and CABUL in the second. The whole is surmounted by a crown and the date 1842 appears below the wreaths.
4. The names CANDAHAR, GHUZNEE and CABUL and the date 1842 in that order, on four lines. Again, the whole is surrounded by a laurel wreath and surmounted by a crown.

The medal was designed by W. Wyon and the ribbon, 1.75in wide, is rainbow-pattern watered red, white, yellow, white and blue. There is a straight steel suspender pinned to a steel clip fastened to the medal. Some of these medals are named in script, others in indented capitals and some are unnamed.

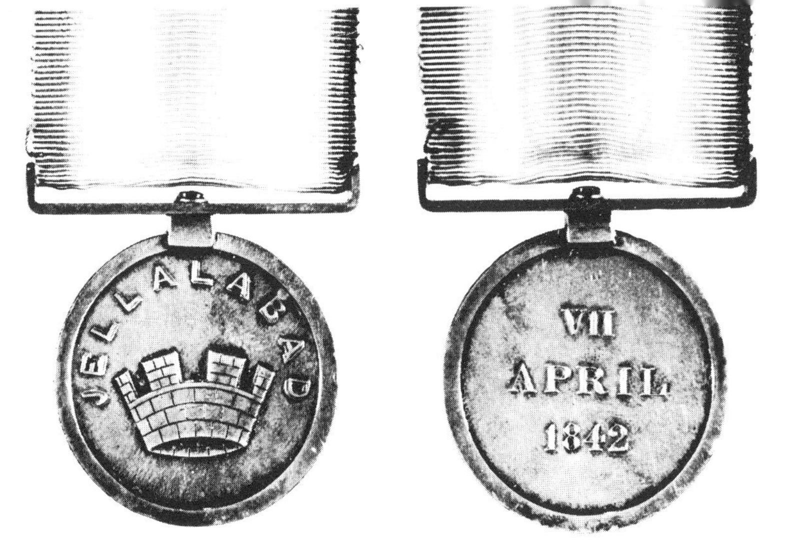

7. Jellalabad Medals 12th November 1841–7th April 1842. First Afghan War.

These medals commemorate the defence of Jellalabad by a small British and Indian force who not only had to contend with besieging Afghans, but also short rations, treason and a number of earthquake shocks which demolished a third of the town and some of the defences. The first medal was approved by a General Order from Allahabad dated 30th April 1842 and was minted in Calcutta. It is generally known as the 'Mural Crown' since the obverse shows a mural crown superscribed JELLALABAD and the reverse has the date VII APRIL 1842 in three lines. The siege was abandoned on this date after a determined attack by the besieged on the Afghan lines. This medal may be found with either a straight steel suspender fitted directly to the rim of the piece, or held by a ring fitted to the medal. The style of naming varies considerably and, in addition, may be named on the edge or on the obverse under the crown. It appears, therefore, that the medal was originally issued unnamed.

The appearance of the second medal, generally referred to as 'Flying Victory', was apparently due to the fact that insufficient of the first type had been minted and, in addition, the Governor-General of India was dissatisfied with the rather crude design. Accordingly, a second medal was designed by W. Wyon and struck at the Royal Mint. The obverse carries the diademed head of Queen Victoria with the legend VICTORIA VINDEX (a few medals were struck with the legend VICTORIA REGINA). The reverse shows the winged figure of Victory with wreaths in her right hand and the staff of a Union Jack in her left hand whilst flying over the fortress of Jellalabad. Following the curve of the upper half circle of the medal is the inscription JELLALABAD VII APRIL and below in the exergue is the date MDCCCXLII. The recipient's name and regiment are indented on the edge in block capitals. The ribbon, common to both types, is rainbow-pattern watered red, yellow, white and blue, 1.75in wide. The Flying Victories were issued in March 1845 and could be exchanged for the earlier issue; few, however, appear to have availed themselves of the offer.

8. Defence of Kelat-I-Ghilzie February–May 1842

Kelat-i-Ghilzie was a fort between Cabul and Candahar, garrisoned by some 900 men, mostly Indians, who were besieged for four months. On the obverse of the medal a laurel wreath surmounted by a mural crown, encloses an ornamental shield which bears the name KELAT I GHILZIE in three lines. The reverse shows a trophy of arms which includes a cuirass, surmounted by a caribinier's helmet, above a plaque inscribed INVICTA MDCCCXLII. The general appearance is Victoriana run amok. The ribbon, 1.75in wide, is rainbow-pattern watered red, white, yellow, white and blue and passes through a straight suspender pinned to an ugly clip sweated to the top of the medal. The recipient's name and regiment are engraved in script on the edge. This is a rare medal when named to a verified recipient. There are a number of unnamed and specimen medals on the market.

9. First China War 5th July 1840–29th August 1842

The 'Opium War' as it is popularly known has a fine, dramatic ring, and conjures up visions of Great Britain trying to stop the rascally heathens from slowly killing themselves with drugs. Unfortunately, the reverse is true and in 1839 it was the Chinese Government which outlawed the importation of opium into their Empire. By way of underlining the edict storage warehouses full of opium, subsequently valued at £3,000,000 were destroyed, and the irate owners refused compensation. In the war that followed, the traditional Chinese fire-breathing dragon heads mounted on the prows of their war junks to terrorise the enemy failed to have the desired effect, and papier mâché dragons came a poor second to British broadsides. The China coastline was completely blockaded and at one point the Emperor of China offered a bounty of 40,000 Chinese dollars for every Englishman, dead or alive. Both the British Commissioner and the Commodore of the British fleet carried a bonus of an extra 10,000 dollars! Amongst the spoils at the end of the war was the island of Hong Kong, ceded in perpetuity, and five trading bases, of which the principal two were Canton and Shanghai.

William Wyon's original, uninhibited design for the campaign medal consisted of a Chinese dragon being savaged by a British lion. More sensitive feelings prevailed, however, and the final reverse shows the arms of England superimposed on a trophy of arms against a palm tree. Above is the inscription ARMIS EXPOSCERE PACEM and in the exergue the word CHINA with the date 1842 underneath. The obverse carries the diademed head of Queen Victoria with the legend VICTORIA REGINA. The medal is worn by a wide (1.5in) crimson ribbon with yellow edges from a straight German silver suspender sweated directly onto the medal. The naming is in bold capitals and the blank spaces filled with stars, similar to the Waterloo medal.

10. Scinde Campaign Medals 6th January–24th March 1843

This campaign against the Amirs of Scinde was a direct result of the preceding Afghan War. On 17th February, Major General Sir Charles Napier commanding 2,800 men and 12 guns attacked, and in three hours defeated, 30,000 Scindian infantry supported by 5,000 cavalry and 15 guns. A month later Sir Charles Napier with 5,000 troops attacked and routed the remainder of the enemy, estimated at 20,000 strong, who were entrenched at Duppa, near Hyderabad. The result was the annexation of Scinde and, what was undoubtedly more important to the troops, substantial prize money as the result of vast booty found in the Amirs' palaces. Sir Charles Napier's share amounted to £68,000. The only British regiment present at both engagements was the 22nd Foot (Cheshires) who lost over 200 men killed and wounded.

In common with some of the earlier Indian Campaign awards there are three different strikings of this silver medal, but only the reverses differ. The obverse in each case shows the diademed head of Queen Victoria and the legend VICTORIA REGINA. The lettering on the reverse, in every instance, is surmounted by a crown and surrounded by a wreath.

1. The name MEEANEE above the date 1842.
2. HYDERABAD above the date 1842.
3. MEEANEE HYDERABAD and the date 1843 in three lines, in that order.

The ribbon is 1.75in wide, rainbow-pattern watered red, white, yellow, white and blue and suspended from a large ring or a straight suspender pinned through a steel clip sweated to the medal. The naming is in block capitals or script, but occasionally medals are found unnamed.

11. Gwalior Campaign Stars December 1843

These stars commemorate two battles fought on the same day, in one of the shortest campaigns ever recorded, against the Mahratta state of Gwalior. The major engagement centred around the village of Maharajpoor where some 18,000 Mahrattas were strongly entrenched with 100 guns. The British army under Sir Hugh Gough was slightly inferior in numbers and decidedly so in artillery, having about 40 guns. The enemy were finally driven from their position after severe hand-to-hand fighting, despite the gallantry of the Gwalior artillerymen who in many cases were bayoneted as they continued to serve the guns. British casualities were about 800 killed and wounded. On the same afternoon, the left wing of the army attacked and routed a small division of the enemy from their position in the hills near Punniar.

The award is a bronze six-pointed star, 1.7in wide and 2in high, made from captured cannon, with a smaller silver centrepiece of similar pattern. In the centre of the small star is the date 29TH

DECR in two lines and in a circle around the date is the name of the action, either PUNNIAR or MAHARAJPOOR and the year 1843. When first issued these stars were fitted with brass hooks and the apparent intention was that they should be worn on the breast of the jacket. Subsequently, many recipients appear to have fitted their own type of suspension, either a straight suspender pinned to the top point of the star or a large ring. Presumably at the same time and quite unofficially, the habit arose of also wearing the star from a ribbon, similar to the Scinde ribbon. The reverse of the star is blank and used for the name and regiment of the recipient, usually in script.

12. Sutlej Campaign Medal 18th December 1845–22nd February 1846. The Sikh Wars

In December 1845 one of the most formidable native powers in India, the Sikh army, trained and in many cases officered by Europeans and supported by excellent artillery, invaded British India. General Gough's army, after a forced march of 150 miles, encountered the Sikh forces, which outnumbered the British by five-to-one, at Moodkee. After heavy fighting and severe losses on both sides, the Sikh army withdrew leaving seventeen guns in British hands. Three days later, on 21st December, reinforced by two battalions of British troops, General Gough moved forward to attack the main Sikh position at Ferozeshuhur. Again the Sikhs resisted ferociously and in the two days' battle that followed the British forces lost one in six of their fighting strength before the enemy was finally defeated. A month later, another Sikh army, having crossed the border, was brought to bay at the village of Aliwal. The British force, outnumbered by two-to-one, was commanded by Sir Harry Smith, later to wear twelve clasps on his Military General Service Medal. The engagement lasted three hours before the Sikhs were routed leaving all their artillery on the field. The 16th Lancers particularly distinguished themselves by charging and breaking an enemy square (losing over 100 men in the process).

The last action of this campaign was fought on the 10th February 1846 at Sobraon where the Sikhs held two miles of entrenchments with 34,000 men, supported by 70 guns and 20,000 reserves. Only about two-fifths of Sir Hugh Gough's army were Europeans, the remainder being native troops. Once again the Sikh army fled in disorder, struggling to escape over the only bridge which spanned the Sutlej river. Finally, the parapet of the bridge collapsed under the press of fugitives and thousands were drowned.

The obverse of the silver medal for this campaign is similar to that of the First China War. The reverse shows the standing figure of Victory with a wreath in her right hand and an olive branch in her left. At her feet is a pile of captured trophies and around the circumference is the legend ARMY OF THE SUTLEJ.

Because the first action in which the recipient fought is given in the exergue, there are four different exergues containing either (1) MOODKEE 1845; (2) FEROZESHUHUR 1845; (3) ALIWAL 1846; or (4) SOBRAON 1846. Three bars were issued, each bearing the name of one of the last three battles. Thus a man who had been in every action received a medal with the exergue MOODKEE 1845, plus three bars. Conversely, a recipient who had been engaged in only the last encounter received a medal with the exergue SOBRAON 1846, without bars. The suspension is an ornamental swivelling suspender and the ribbon dark blue with crimson edges. Naming is impressed in capital letters or Roman skeleton lettering.

13. South African Campaigns 1834–1853

This medal was sanctioned on 22nd November 1854 for survivors of the three campaigns against the Kaffirs in South Africa during the years 1834-1835, 1846-1847 and 1850-1853. As this award is dated 1853 it must have been just as confusing for the recipients who earned it in 1843 as it is for collectors today. The only way of determining the campaign for which the medal was awarded is to check the recipient against the regimental roll. Even this is not possible with medals issued to the Naval Brigade which often only show the name and rank. An interesting point connected with these wars is that the wife of Sir Harry Smith (veteran of the Peninsular, India, and Governor of the Colony) was to give her name to a town made famous during the South African War–Ladysmith. Another famous incident connected with the later campaign was the sinking of the troopship *'Birkenhead'* with the officers and men drawn up in parade order on the deck, after the women, children and sick had been safely placed in the boats. Their heroism so impressed King William of Prussia that he ordered an account of the disaster to be read to every unit in the German Army.

The obverse of the medal and suspender is similar to the Punjab award (Medal No. 14), whilst the reverse shows a lion, stopping to drink in front of a bush. Above him are the words SOUTH AFRICA and in the exergue the date 1853. The ribbon is watered orange with two wide and two narrow dark blue stripes. The obverse was designed by W. Wyon and the reverse by L.C. Wyon. The naming is indented in Roman capitals.

---

14. Punjab Campaign Medal 7th September 1848–14th March 1849

This campaign was virtually a continuation of the Sutlej War which had left the militant Sikhs in a state of unrest. The Punjab flared into rebellion in 1848 and the British fielded two armies; one 28,000 strong under Major General Whish besieged the rebel stronghold of Mooltan whilst the second, under Lord Gough, turned northwards towards the Punjab. On 13th January Gough reached Chilianwala where a Sikh army under Sher Singh was entrenched. In the savage battle that followed, where both sides slaughtered the enemy wounded, the British lost several colours, four guns and over 15 per cent of their effective strength. Heaviest casualties were suffered by the South Wales

Borderers who lost 21 officers and 503 other ranks killed or wounded. Both sides withdrew to their respective camps where they were bogged down by three days of torrential rain. However, on 22nd January, Mooltan had been stormed and Whish's troops moved northward to support Gough. Sher Singh struck his camp and moved eastward making for Lahore but on 20th February the combined British forces, totalling 24,000 men and 96 guns caught up with the Sikhs at Goojerat. The battle started at 7am and by early afternoon the enemy were in full retreat, abandoning their guns, wounded and baggage.

A General Order dated 2nd April 1849 granted a medal to all forces employed in the Punjab during the campaign. The reverse of this medal is extremely detailed and shows the Sikh army surrendering their arms and colours in front of a mounted officer. Two regiments of East India troops, complete with colours, are drawn up in the middle distance, whilst in the background there are large palm trees on a hill. Around the top is the legend TO THE ARMY OF THE PUNJAB, and in the exergue the date in Roman numerals MDCCCXLIX. The obverse carries the diademed head of Queen Victoria and the ribbon is dark blue with a yellow stripe on each side, threaded through an ornamental swivelling suspender. Three clasps were issued for the main actions–MOOLTAN, for those engaged in the siege from 7th September 1848 until 22nd January 1849 and CHILIANWALA and GOOJERAT for the two main battles. The maximum number of clasps to any one man was two, although there are numerous medals without clasps awarded to troops who did not participate in any of the three main actions. Naming is in impressed Roman capitals.

15. India General Service Medal 1854–1895

The obverse of this medal and the suspender is similar to those on the Punjab medal. The reverse shows the winged figure of Victory crowning a seated warrior. A lotus flower and four leaves appear in the exergue. The junctions of the suspender, clasp and all the bars are each covered by a rosette, and there are three equal crimson and blue stripes on the ribbon. Twenty-three bars were issued covering a period of forty-one years as follows:

PEGU 28th March 1852-30th June 1853. The second campaign in Burma.

PERSIA 5th December 1856-8th February 1857. A combined naval and army expedition.

NORTH WEST FRONTIER 3rd December 1849-22nd October 1868. Fifteen different campaigns and expeditions spread over nineteen years.

UMBEYLA 20th October-23rd December 1863. An expeditionary force in Hindustan.

BHOOTAN December 1864-February 1866. A four-column punitive force.

LOOSHAI 9th December 1871-20th February 1872. An expedition to recover an abducted planter and his daughter. No British troops were involved.

PERAK 2nd November 1875-20th March 1876. An expedition to Perak which included a naval brigade

JOWAKI 1877-8 9th November 1877-19th January 1878. The Afridi tribesmen near the Kohat Pass objected to a new road running through their territory.

NAGA 1879-80 December 1879-January 1880. A punitive expedition against the Nagas.

BURMA 1885-7 14th November 1885-30th April 1887. The annexation of Burma.

SIKKIM 1888 15th March-27th September 1888. A three-cornered fight with Sikkim which also involved the Tibetans.

HAZARA 1888. This is generally known as the Black Mountain Expedition.

BURMA 1887-89 1st May 1887-31st March 1889. Chiefly this involved the suppression of quite large scale banditry, a left-over from the earlier Burma campaign.

CHIN LUSHAI 1889-90 15th November 1889-30th April 1890. This was earned by two columns, the Burma column operating against the Chins and the Chittagong column in action with the Lushais.

SAMANA 1891 5th April-25th May 1891. This was awarded for operations in the Miranzai Valley and the Samana Heights.

HAZARA 1891 12th March-16th May 1891. This was for the Hazara Field Force in the Black Mountains.

N.E. FRONTIER 1891 28th March-7th May 1891. This clasp was earned by the Manipur Field Force dealing with the obstreperous Rajah of Manipur, a small state adjoining Assam and Burma.

HUNZA 1891 1st-22 December 1891. A small but hard-fought campaign which resulted in three Victoria Crosses.

BURMA 1889-92 This was for eleven punitive expeditions, some only lasting a few days.

LUSHAI 1889-92 11th January 1889-8th June 1892. This was awarded for small expeditions into the Lushai Hills.

CHIN HILLS 1892-93 19th October 1892-10th March 1893. A small punitive expedition against the Chins.

KACHIN HILLS 1892-93 3rd December 1892-3rd March 1893. This was for punitive expeditions into the Kachin Hills.

WAZIRISTAN 1894-95 22nd October 1894-13th March 1895. A fairly large expedition against the Wazirs and a portent of several more against the same tribes.

A wide variety of naming. Medals with the last twelve bars were issued in bronze to native noncombatants.

16. Crimean War Medal 28th March 1854–30th March 1856

A monkish squabble over the custody of keys to a church in the Holy Land was the ostensible cause which led to the death of many thousands of men and living misery for the remainder, who soldiered in conditions unequalled until the bloody quagmires of World War I. The official declaration of war was made on 28th March 1854 and in the summer the British and French forces reached Varna in Bulgaria. The Russians promptly withdrew and the allies were left with a problem of finding the enemy. Consequently, in September the Allied Army sailed for the Crimea with a loose directive to take Sebastopol, the Russian base. On 20th September 1854 the Russians, entrenched on the heights above the Alma river, were attacked and defeated. In the war that followed fleas, flies and fever, coupled with sunstroke in summer and frostbite in winter, killed more British troops than the entire Russian army. Of the 20,425 other ranks fatalities only 1,933 died of wounds

and 2,598 were killed in action; the remaining 15,894 died of disease. The remaining battles are well known– Balaklava on 25th October 1854; the magnificent charge of Scarlett's Heavy Brigade and the equally magnificent, but useless, charge of the Light Brigade; Inkermann, the 'Soldier's Battle' fought in fog and mist against overwhelming odds on 5th November 1854; and finally, the long weary siege of Sebastopol, culminating in its capture on 9th September 1855. Hostilities were then virtually suspended until peace was signed on 29th March 1856. The futile war was over.

In December 1854 whilst the war was still in progress, the Queen commanded that a medal be awarded to all ranks engaged in the Crimea, with the addition of clasps for Alma or Inkermann for troops engaged at those battles. A clasp was granted for Balaklava in February 1855 and in the following October a further clasp for Sebastopol. Naval forces who operated in the Sea of Azoff were granted a clasp bearing the word AZOFF. The reverse of the medal depicts the winged figure of Victory crowning a Roman warrior with a laurel wreath; the word CRIMEA is inscribed to the left of the figures. On the obverse is the diademed head of Queen Victoria with the legend VICTORIA REGINA round the sides and the date 1854 underneath. The clasps are in the shape of oak leaves, with acorn ornaments, attached to a foliated suspender peculiar to this medal; the ribbon is light blue with yellow edges. Medals were originally issued unnamed but could be returned for naming free of charge in indented capitals. Although a total of five clasps was issued not more than four will be found on any one medal. Medals will be seen bearing single clasps for ALMA, AZOFF or SEBASTOPOL, but anyone entitled to either BALAKLAVA or INKERMANN automatically qualified for SEBASTOPOL. This included members of the Naval Brigade serving ashore. Medals with four clasps to cavalrymen who charged with the Light Brigade are highly prized (and priced) and so, to a lesser extent, are similar medals to the Heavy Brigade.

17. Baltic Medal March 1854–August 1855

After a Fleet Review at Spithead on 23rd April 1856 the Queen commanded that a medal should be awarded to the officers and men of the Royal Navy who had served in the Baltic from March 1854 until the blockade was lifted in 1855. The obverse of the medal is similar to that of the Crimea, except that the date is omitted. On the reverse is a seated figure of Britannia holding a trident and looking over her left shoulder. Behind her are the Russian fortresses of Bormarsund and Sveaborg, while in the foreground is a naval cannon with a pyramid of shot. The word BALTIC is shown around the top and the dates 1854-1855 appear in the exergue. No clasps were awarded, and the ribbon is yellow with blue edges. Apart from about 100 medals awarded to the Royal Sappers and Miners who served on ships, the medal was issued unnamed and is not highly valued. Many recipients, however, had their medals engraved at their own expense, usually including the name of the ship on which they served.

18. India Mutiny Medal 1857–1858

It is well known that greased cartridges started the Indian Mutiny, but like all well known fairy stories it is not quite true. Whilst the Enfield cartridge may have provided the flashpoint, India was already ripe for an explosion in the spring of 1857. The first outbreak occurred at Merrut on Sunday 10th May 1857 and spread throughout Bengal with the holy men prophesying a return of the Mogul dynasty. No doubt readers will be familiar with the main outlines of the rebellion, and the retribution that followed, but two episodes will always be remembered. One was the deliberate action of Conductor Scully, who blew himself and 1,000 mutineers to eternity when he fired the main powder magazine at Delhi; the other is the 'massacre of the innocents' at Cawnpore and the aftermath–one of the few recorded occasions when British troops refused to give quarter. The five main actions for which clasps were subsequently awarded are as follows:

DELHI 30th May-14th September 1857. To troops employed in the re-capture of that city.

DEFENCE OF LUCKNOW 29th June-22nd November 1857. To the original defenders, including about 160 co-opted or volunteer civilians, and also to the first relief force under Havelock.

RELIEF OF LUCKNOW November 1857. To Sir Colin Campbell's force engaged in the relief of the city; these included a British Naval Brigade.

LUCKNOW November 1857-March 1858. Awarded to all forces engaged in the capture of Lucknow.

CENTRAL INDIA January-June 1858. Covered numerous battles and engagements involving the Rajpatana Field Force and the Madras Column. Also for operations in and around Jhansi, Calpee and Gwalior.

In 1858 the Indian Government granted a medal to all armed forces of the Crown and the Honourable East India Company. Two years later the award was extended to all who had borne arms in the suppression of mutiny, including civilians. The obverse of the medal is similar to the Baltic medal. The reverse shows the standing, helmeted figure of Britannia holding a laurel wreath in her outstretched right hand. Over her left arm is the Union Shield and her left hand holds other wreaths (apparently for distribution to the victorious troops). Behind her is a standing British lion and the word INDIA above.

The dates 1857-1858 appear in the exergue. An unusual and ornamental suspender carries the ribbon which has alternate white and red stripes (three of white and two red). The colours are popularly believed to be red for blood and white symbolising the massacred innocents. The recipient's name and unit, or ship, is impressed on the edge in Roman capitals. Although five bars were authorised, the maximum to any one man was four and these only to certain cavalry regiments. Infantry, including the Naval Brigade, could not earn more than two and many medals were issued without clasps. Unlike many mid-Victorian campaign medals, the Indian Mutiny medal was only awarded for service under fire.

19. Second China War Medal 1857–1860

As far as military historians are concerned the events in China during 1857-8 rank as the second China War. whilst the campaign in 1860 is known as the third China War. However, medal collectors invariably refer to the whole as the second China War because one award covered the three years. (In case this sounds rather complicated, a contemporary account quotes a corporal of the Buffs as referring 'to another do with them bloody yellow "eathen",' so presumably there have always been different points of view among nomenclators). The first fighting was between naval forces but in 1860 the British and French landed forces which began to fight their way overland towards the Taku Forts. During this advance a private soldier of the Buffs, No. 2051 John Moyse, who was in charge of sixteen coolies carrying the rum ration for the force, was captured by Tartar cavalry. The incident that followed, when Moyse refused to kowtow to a mandarin and was beheaded in consequence, made the front page of 'The Times', earned his name a place in the Buffs Regimental Museum and immortalized him in the famous poem by Sir Francis Doyle.

The Taku Forts were successfully stormed on the 21st August 1860 during which the attackers won seven V.C.s. The Chinese, especially their artillerymen, appear to have fought very well, despite stories in English newspapers that they were tied to their guns to prevent them escaping. (Similar tales made the rounds in 1918 about German heavy machine-gun crews). The expeditionary force fought two more quite severe actions before taking Pekin on 13th October 1860. A well directed campaign was somewhat marred by the loss of the Summer Palace in Pekin which the French looted and the British then burned to the ground.

A General Order dated 6th March 1861 awarded a medal to all services engaged in the operations. The obverse is similar to the Indian Mutiny medal whilst the reverse shows the Royal Arms superimposed against a trophy of arms (which appears to include chain shot) in front of a palm tree. Above is the inscription ARMIS EXPOSCERE PACEM and the word CHINA in the exergue. A horn shaped suspender carries the ribbon which was originally multicoloured with five equally spaced stripes of blue, yellow, red, white and green. A number of medals were certainly issued with this ribbon, but it was later changed to one of crimson with yellow edges. Awards to the Royal Navy were not named, but those to soldiers and marines are named in indented Roman capitals. Six clasps were authorised, the first of which, CHINA 1842 is something of a mystery as a medal had already been awarded for that campaign. Of the remaining five, FATSHAN 1857 and TAKU FORTS 1858 could only be earned by Naval personnel, including marines. The other three clasps were CANTON 1857, TAKU FORTS 1860 and PEKIN 1860. The greatest number of clasps to any one man was five, on a medal to Thomas Cole of the Royal Marine Artillery.

C

20. New Zealand Medal 1845–1847 and 1860–1866

This award was sanctioned on 1st March 1869, for issue to survivors of those engaged in suppressing the Maori risings in North Island between 1845 and 1846, those in the South Island during 1847 and service generally in New Zealand between 1860 and 1866. It is impossible to itemise the various encounters and engagements; suffice it to say that the Maori proved a worthy and gallant foe and one whose fortified stockades were impregnable to everything except artillery fire. No less than twenty-nine different reverses were struck for this medal, twenty-eight of them bearing different dates, and one undated.

The obverse of the medal shows the head of Queen Victoria, wearing a coronet which holds a veil covering the back of her neck. Around the head is the legend VICTORIA D : G : BRITT : REG : F : D :. On the reverse is a small laurel wreath which surrounds the date or dates of service. Above are the words NEW ZEALAND and below VIRTUTIS HONOR. Any one of the following dates is shown: 1845-46; 1845-47; 1846-47; 1846; 1847; 1848; 1860; 1860-61; 1860-63; 1860-64; 1860-65; 1860-66; 1861; 1861-63; 1861-64; 1861-65; 1861-66; 1862-66; 1863; 1863-64; 1863-65; 1863-66; 1864; 1864-65; 1864-66; 1865; 1865-66; and 1866. A straight ornamental swivelling suspender, supposed to be fashioned after a fern frond, carried the dark blue ribbon with $^3/_8$in wide red centre stipe. This is a difficult medal to verify as it was not awarded for any particular engagement, but for service in an area during a period of time. In particular, no official actions are recorded between 6th November 1861 and 4th May 1863 but medals were issued bearing, or including, these dates.

21. Canada General Service Medal 1866–1870

Thirty-three years after the first raid, an Army Order of January 1899 authorised the Canadian Government to issue a medal to members of the Imperial forces and Canadian Militia who had been engaged in the Fenian Raids and the Red River Expedition under Colonel Wolseley. At the end of the American Civil War the Fenians (sworn to liberate Ireland from the yoke of England) decided to start their programme by liberating Canada. The invading army, numbers uncertain, under O'Neill, proved no match for the Canadian Militia and were hustled back over the U.S. border, where many of them were arrested. The second raid coincided with a rebellion led by self-styled 'General' Louis Reil, whose supporters occupied Fort Garry, imprisoned many residents and seized the Hudson Bay Company's treasury. The second Fenian raid promptly dispersed when confronted by the Canadian Militia and the rebellion collapsed on the arrival of Imperial and Canadian forces. Reil escaped however, and was responsible for a second rebellion fifteen years later.

On the obverse of the medal is a veiled bust of Queen Victoria with the legend VICTORIA REGINA ET IMPERATRIX. The reverse shows the Canadian flag surrounded by a maple wreath and above it the word CANADA. The ribbon has equal vertical divisions of red, white and red. Three bars were issued–FENIAN RAID 1866; FENIAN RAID 1870 and RED RIVER 1870 and the medal was never awarded without a bar or bars. Just over 16,000 medals were issued, but only 20 of these carried all three bars. Naming is usually impressed in square capitals.

22. Abyssinian War Medal 4th October 1867–19th April 1868

Theodore, King of Abyssinia, having imprisoned and held in chains a number of British and German subjects, including the British Consul, it became necessary to point out the error of his ways. The expeditionary force under Sir Robert Napier was extremely well organized, particularly regarding transport and medical facilities, and the camp followers and drivers far exceeded in numbers the 14,000 troops, including a naval brigade. This is a disappointing award for those who like 'blood' on their medals as the total British casualties amounted to 66, of whom 29 were wounded and the remaining 37 died of disease.

The medal, authorised by a General Order dated 1st March 1869, is very distinctive and much smaller than usual (1.25in diameter). The obverse shows a coroneted and veiled bust of Queen Victoria within a beaded circle and surrounded by a nine-pointed star. Between each angle of the points is one of the letters of the word ABYSSINIA.

On the reverse, in a beaded circle surrounded by a wreath of laurel, is embossed the recipient's name, rank and unit or ship. The medal is suspended from a silver swivel ring attached to a crown soldered to the top of the piece. The ribbon is 1.5in wide, white, with a broad red stripe down the centre.

Recipients' details were die-struck in the centre of the obverse, but medals awarded to Indian troops had this information engraved or impressed.

23. Ashantee War Medal
9th June 1873–4th February 1874

This medal, authorised on 1st June 1874, was awarded for Sir Garnet Wolseley's campaign against the Ashanti in the Gold Coast, or Ghana as it is now known. Again the casualties were very light and disease incapacitated far more troops than the enemy. This was the only occasion when the Martini-Henry Elcho bayonet was used on active service. A 20in blade swelling to a double-edged spear point with saw serrations on the back edge, this was supposed to serve a double purpose in both killing the enemy and clearing a passage through the undergrowth.

On the obverse of the piece is the legend VICTORIA REGINA above the diademed head of Queen Victoria, wearing a veil. The reverse is filled to capacity with bodies and branches, allegedly British troops fighting natives in the bush. The ribbon is 1.25in wide, yellow with black borders and two thin black stripes down the centre. The naming is in indented capitals and the date 1873-4 is also shown. One bar COOMASSIE was awarded to all those who crossed the River Prah and also troops engaged in either of the actions at Amoaful and Ardahsa on 31st January and 4th February 1874 respectively.

24. Zulu and Basuto War Medal 25th September 1877–2nd December 1879

This medal was sanctioned in 1880 and is similar to that for the previous South African campaigns between 1834 and 1853 except for the substitution of a Zulu shield and four crossed assegais for the date in the exergue. The name of the recipient and his unit is engraved on the rim in capital letters. Although it was possible to earn the medal without a bar (for service in Natal between 11th January and 1st September 1879) it was usually issued with one of five dated bars–1877-8 for actions against the Galekas; 1878 for operations involving the Griquas; 1879 the Zulu War or the mopping up operations against Chiefs Sekukini or Moirosi and 1878-9 or 1877-8-9 for men engaged in more than one campaign.

Medals to men who fought in the main actions of the Zulu War (Isandhlwana, Rorke's Drift and Ulundi) usually command a much higher price than awards for the other campaigns. The invasion of Zululand began on 11th January 1879 and despite the fact that the Zulus, under Cetewayo, were one of the most powerful military nations Africa had ever seen (they had defeated the Boers on more than one occasion) the British commander, Lord Chelmsford, seems to have grossly underestimated his enemy.

One of the invading columns halted at Isandhlwana, some miles inside Zululand, but no attempt was made to fortify the temporary camp. On 22nd January 1879 it was attacked by a Zulu army of about 14,000 men led by Dambulamanzi, Cetewayo's half-brother, and the invaders massacred almost to a man. Elated by their success, part of the Zulu army moved down the Tugela river where, on the Natal side, stood two stone buildings with thatched roofs. Originally a Swedish mission station and now doing duty as a military hospital and store depot, the name of the post was to become part of British military history–Rorke's Drift. The small garrison began building a parapet of biscuit boxes but this was only two boxes high when the first Zulu attack was launched at 4-30pm. Time and time again throughout the night waves of Zulu warriors attempted to storm the post. Finally, at dawn the next morning, the enemy withdrew leaving over 400 of their dead on or around the post. The garrison had lost 17 men killed and 5 of their sick men burned to death when the hospital was fired. They had also won eight Victoria Crosses, including one to Corporal Scheiss of the Natal Native Contingent, originally a patient in the hospital and the only Swiss national ever to gain this award. News of Isandhlwana meanwhile created a sensation in England and strong reinforcements were hurried out to the Cape. However, even before they reached the front the Zulus suffered a crushing defeat at Ulundi. Cetewayo's retreat was turned into a rout by three squadrons of the 17th Lancers, supported by mounted infantry and volunteers, who pursued the beaten army for seven miles.

25. Afghanistan 1878–1880

The causes of the second Afghan war in the 'training ground' of the British Army are too many to enumerate here; suffice it to say that Afghanistan was invaded by three British columns who fought a series of actions. In one of these, at the battle of Maiwand on 27th July 1880, a British and Indian force was overwhelmed by Afghans and the survivors besieged in Kandahar. This defeat was lightened by the gallantry of the 66th Foot (Royal Berkshires) who covered the retreat of the remainder of the column until only eleven men were left on their feet. Surrounded by 10,000 Afghans and Ghazis and accompanied only by their regimental mascot, a small white dog, these eleven Berkshire men, who had fired all their ammunition, refused to surrender. Instead they charged! Needless to say, the battle of Maiwand (nearly a thousand casualties, most of them killed) did not merit a bar, but the action at Ali Masjid (fourteen killed) earned a clasp and battle honours.

On 19th March 1881 a medal was granted which showed on the obverse the crowned draped bust of Queen Victoria and the legend VICTORIA REGINA ET IMPERATRIX. The reverse is crowded with elephant-borne artillery, mounted and foot soldiers with a fortress-capped mountain in the background. In the top left hand arc is the word AFGHANISTAN and the dates 1878-79-80 in the exergue. The ribbon is green with crimson stripes on each edge. Six bars were authorised but not more than four could be earned by any one man. ALI MUSJID 21st November 1878; PEIWAR KOTAL 2nd December 1878; CHARASIA 6th October 1879; KABUL 10-23 December 1879; AHMED KHEL 19th April 1880 and KANDAHAR 1st September 1880. Medals to British troops were engraved in squat or sloping capitals whilst those issued to natives were named in capitals or sloping script.

26. Kabul to Kandahar Star 9th–31st August 1880

This bronze star, made from captured cannon taken at the battle of Kandahar, was awarded to all who had taken part in General Robert's famous march to relieve Kandahar. It is a five-pointed star with a ball between the inner angles, except the top one. In the centre is the monogram VR1 around which is a circular raised border. In raised lettering on this border are the words KABUL TO KANDAHAR with the date 1880 at the bottom. The reverse is plain with a hollow centre. The star is surmounted by a crown to which is attached a ring, 7/10ths in diameter, which holds the typical India pattern rainbow red, white, yellow, white and blue ribbon. There is engraved naming on the reverse, capital letters for British troops and capitals or sloping script for Indian soldiers.

27. Cape of Good Hope General Service Medal 1880–1897

This medal was issued in 1900 by the Cape Government, with the approval of the Crown, to Colonial troops and a small number of British officers and men who had been engaged in suppressing small risings in the places named on the bars.

The obverse shows the crowned bust of Queen Victoria and the legend VICTORIA REGINA ET IMPERATRIX. On the reverse is the arms of Cape Colony with the motto SPES BONA. The ribbon has equal vertical bands of dark blue, light biscuit and dark blue. The three bars are TRANSKEI 13th September 1880-13th May 1881 for operations in Tembuland and Griqualand East, where the natives refused to hand in their firearms; BASUTOLAND 13th September 1880-27th April 1881 sporadic fighting as a result of which Basutoland became a Crown Colony in March 1884; and BECHUANALAND 24th December 1896-30th July 1897, where a native revolt was suppressed.

---

28. Egypt 1882–1889

Mehemit Ali, Khedive of Egypt, notorious for his women, gambling and what the literature of the period guardedly calls 'unnatural appetites' was obliged to sell his Suez Canal shares to Great Britain. Shortly afterwards he was replaced by his son Tewfik who had inherited all his father's vices and invented some of his own. The state of the country worsened and in 1882 the army, which had not been paid or clothed for several years, mutinied under Arabi Pasha. Arabi threatened to seize the Suez Canal (all this has a familiar ring) and began to strengthen the forts guarding Alexandria. On 11th July 1882 after an ultimatum the British fleet bombarded the fortifications and landed seamen and marines to restore order.

Britain was now committed to restore law and order, and an attack was made on the rebel army who had entrenched themselves at Tel-el-Kebir. Guided by naval officers with compasses the British force made a night march across the desert and routed the enemy. An occupational force of 10,000 men was left in Egypt, and a General Order of 1882 granted a medal with appropriate bars to those engaged in the two battles.

Britain now found herself responsible for a country without revenue, an army or administration. At this awkward moment in time there appeared in the Sudan, nominally ruled by Egypt, the Mahdi or 'Expected One', a religious fanatic whose puritanical control over his dervishes

would have made Cromwell green with envy. To suppress the rebellion an Egyptian army of some 10,000 led by Hicks Pasha marched out against the dervishes. Although the force looked impressive on paper, many of the men had been released from prison following their part in the 1882 mutiny and 51 men of the Krupp battery managed to desert en route although chained to their guns. The result was a foregone conclusion and at the beginning of November the army was slaughtered and all their guns and nearly a million rounds of ammunition fell into the hands of the Mahdi. After a series of further engagements the British Government decided to withdraw from the Sudan. 'Chinese' Gordon was appointed to undertake the evacuation of garrisons and civil staff, but by the end of 1884 Gordon was besieged in Khartoum. The relief column fought its way up the Nile, only to arrive forty-eight hours too late to prevent the fall of the city and Gordon's murder. During the course of the next five years, eleven more clasps were authorised for the Egypt medal and the medal itself was re-issued in 1884 but with a plain exergue.

The obverse of the medal is similar to that for Ashantee, (No. 23). The first reverse shows a simple design of the Sphinx with the word EGYPT above and the date 1882 below. The ribbon has three bright blue and two white stripes of equal width. Dated medals are engraved in sloping capitals, as are the second issue to British troops. Undated medals issued to Indian troops are engraved in small running script and those awarded to the Egyptian army are named in Arabic. The clasps are as follows:

ALEXANDRIA 11th JULY 1882; TEL-EL-KEBIR 13th September 1882; EL-TEB 29th February 1884; TAMAII 13th March 1884; EL-TEB-TAMAII (To those who took part in both actions); SUAKIN 1884; THE NILE 1884-85 (awarded to those who served in the expedition to relieve Gordon); ABU KLEA 17th January 1885. A savage engagement and the only recorded instance when a British square broke; KIRBEKAN (in common with the previous clasp, this bar is always found in conjunction with that for THE NILE 1884-85); SUAKIN 1885; TOFREK (always found in conjunction with the previous bar); GEMAIZAH 20th December 1888; TOSKI 3rd August 1889.

THE KHEDIVE'S STARS. Five-pointed bronze stars were awarded by the Khedive to all recipients of the Egypt medal.

29. North West Canada 1885

This medal was sanctioned for issue on 18th September 1885 to all who had taken part in the suppression of Riel's Rebellion. Riel, who had escaped from Fort Garry in 1870, set up a provisional government and promised heaven on earth to his supporters, mainly Fenians and local Indians. Most of the Canadian militia wcrc involvcd and thc rising was speedily suppressed. Riel was unable to try the principle of 'third time lucky' as he was expeditiously tried and hanged.

The obverse of the medal is similar to that awarded for the Ashantee War. The reverse has the words NORTH WEST CANADA surrounded by a maple wreath and the date 1885 in the centre. The ribbon is blue-grey in colour with two red stripes two millimetres from each edge. The medals were issued unnamed, but many are found named in block letters. One bar SASKATCHEWAN was awarded to all those who had fought in any of the three main actions of the rebellion, namely at the Saskatchewan and Fish Rivers and Batoche. No British troops were present except for nine officers on the Canadian Staff.

30. East and West Africa 1887–1900

Whilst this medal is slightly thinner than that issued for the Ashantee campaign of 1873-74, (plate 23), it is otherwise identical, even to the ribbon and suspension. Recipients of the Ashantee medal only gained the appropriate bar for further service in East and West Africa between the dates shown, and not another medal. Twenty-three bars were authorised but for some peculiar reason the M'wele campaign in 1895-96 failed to qualify for a bar; instead the name and date were engraved round the rim. The bars are as follows:

1887-8 13th November 1887-2nd January 1888. For operations against the Tonnie Tribe.

WITU 1890 17th-27th October 1890. A punitive expedition against the Sultan of Witu.

1891-2 29th December 1891-2nd February 1892. An expedition to Gambia.

1892 8th March-25th May 1892. Expeditions against Tambi, Toniataba and the Jebus.

WITU AUGUST 1893 7th-13th August 1893. More trouble with the Sultan of Witu.

LIWONDI 1893 February-March 1893. A small naval force against Chief Liwondi.

JUBA RIVER 1893 23rd-25th August 1893. A small volunteer force against the Somalis.

LAKE NYASSA 1893 November 1893. Another volunteer boat party against a local chief.

1893-94 16th November 1893-11th March 1894. Operations in Sierra Leone and Gambia.

GAMBIA 1894 23rd February-13th March 1894. This commemorates some heavy fighting and casualties for the naval brigade involved.

BENIN RIVER 1894 August-September 1894. An expedition chiefly naval, up the Benin River.

BRASS RIVER 1895 17th-26th February 1895. Operations against King Koko.

1896-98 27th November 1896-27th June 1898. This was awarded for several punitive expeditions into the Northern Territories of the Gold Coast.

NIGER 1897 6th January-26th February. An expedition to Western Provinces.

BENIN 1897 6th February-7th August. A punitive column to Benin territory.

DAWKITA 1897 28th March 1897. The defence of Dawkita against Sofa tribesmen, in the Gold Coast.

1897-98 September 1897-August 1898. Expeditions, chiefly against the Ebos by Lagos Frontier Force.

1898. Conditions similar to the previous bar.

SIERRA LEONE 1898-99 18th February 1898-9th March 1899. Two expeditions involving native troops and a naval brigade.

1899 February-May 1899. Expeditions in Southern Nigeria.

1900 4th January-8th May 1900. An expedition to Kaduna and against the Munshis in the Northern Province.

31. British South Africa Company's Medal 1890–1897

There are four different reverses to this award, although the obverse is the same in each case, namely the bust of Queen Victoria, crowned and veiled, with the legend VICTORIA REGINA. The reverse shows a speared charging lion with a native shield and spears in the foreground. Below, in two lines, are the words BRITISH SOUTH AFRICA COMPANY. Above is the name and date of the campaign: 1. MATABELELAND 1893; 2. RHODESIA 1896; 3. MASHONALAND 1897 and 4. no place or date, which was authorised for the Mashonaland campaign of 1890. The first medal was sanctioned by Queen Victoria in 1896; the last was authorised by King George V in 1927–thirty-seven years after the incident. The medal is larger than usual and is 1.45in in diameter. The ribbon is 1.4in wide and orange-yellow with three narrow blue stripes, one in the centre and one 3mm from each edge. The suspender is an ornate affair, too wide for the ribbon, and is a mass of roses, shamrocks and thistles.

Four bars were issued:

MASHONALAND 1890. More in the nature of a flag and survey expedition.

MATABELELAND 1893. The first Matabele War including Major Wilson's epic stand with thirty men on the Shangani River.

RHODESIA 1896. Small scale revolts by the Matabele and Mashona tribes.

MASHONALAND 1897. A fairly large rebellion and heavy fighting.

32. Central Africa 1891–189

This medal is identical on both the obverse and reverse with the East and West Africa medal (No. 30) previously described. The ribbon has vertical equal bands of black, white and terracotta, suspended by means of a small swivelling ring affixed to a claw at the top of the medal. Naming varies. The medal was first issued to commemorate a number of small campaigns in Central and East Africa between 1891 and 1894. It was re-issued in 1899 for operations in British Central Africa between 1894 and 1898. On the last occasion it was fitted with a plain suspender and a bar CENTRAL AFRICA 1894-98 was added. Men who had already received the first issue received only the bar and had the rings removed from their original medal and replaced by the straight suspender.

33. India Medal 1895 – 1902

The obverse of this medal is similar to plate 21 (the Canada General Service award), whilst the reverse shows a British and an Indian soldier both supporting the same flag. The word INDIA is on the left and the date 1895 on the right. The ornamental suspender and rosettes are the same type as those fitted to the India General Service 1854 medal and the ribbon has three vertical bands of crimson and two of dark green, interspaced. These awards were generally named in script except for the Highland Light Infantry whose medals were named in block capitals. Seven bars were issued, but as Queen Victoria died before the issue of the seventh, the medal was re-struck. This second issue shows the bust of King Edward VII in Field Marshal's uniform and the legend EDWARVS VII REX IMPERATOR. In all other respects it is the same as the first issue. All these medals were awarded in bronze to native non-combatants.

The bars are as follows:

DEFENCE OF CHITRAL 1895 3rd March-19th April 1895. A seven week siege of a small garrison.

RELIEF OF CHITRAL 1895 7th March-15th August 1895. For the Relief column which fought through to the garrison.

PUNJAB FRONTIER 1897-98 10th June 1897-6th April 1898. For the defenders of Shabkadr Fort, Mohmand Field Force and Tirah Expeditionary Force.

MALAKAND 1897 26th July-2nd August 1897. For the defence and relief of Chakdara and Malakand.

SAMANA 1897 22nd August-2nd October 1897. For operations on Samana Ridge defence of Fort Gulistan and the 21 Sikh defenders of Saragai post who held off 10,000 Afridis for four days before being overrun and massacred.

TIRAH 1897-98 2nd October 1897-6th April 1898. This bar, never issued singly, was awarded to the Tirah Expeditionary Force which included the Kurram and Peshawar Columns and the Rawalpindi Brigade. Troops on lines of communications and the Swat Valley also received this bar, and as the principle Afridi amusement was attacking convoys it was well earned. Unlike the handful of casualties behind many of the campaign bars, Tirah commemorates over 300 killed and nearly a thousand wounded.

WAZIRISTAN 1901-2 23rd November 1901-10th March 1902. The bar was awarded with the second issue medal for four months of roadmaking, fighting and raids against the Mahsuds.

34. Ashanti Star 1896 7th December 1895–17th January 1896

Further trouble on the Gold Coast, including torture, cannibalism, human sacrifices and other unneighbourly behaviour led to the Ashanti Expedition, comprising about 2,000 troops. A distinctive gun metal star was awarded for this campaign consisting of a four-pointed star bisected by a St. Andrew's Cross. In the centre is the Imperial crown surrounded by a raised band inscribed ASHANTI on top and the date 1896 below. On the reverse, in raised lettering, are the words FROM THE QUEEN. The star is suspended by means of a ring attached to the top of the upper point, and the ribbon is yellow with a black stripe 2mm from each edge. It was issued unnamed, but the 2nd Battalion of the West Yorkshire Regiment had their awards named at their Colonel's expense.

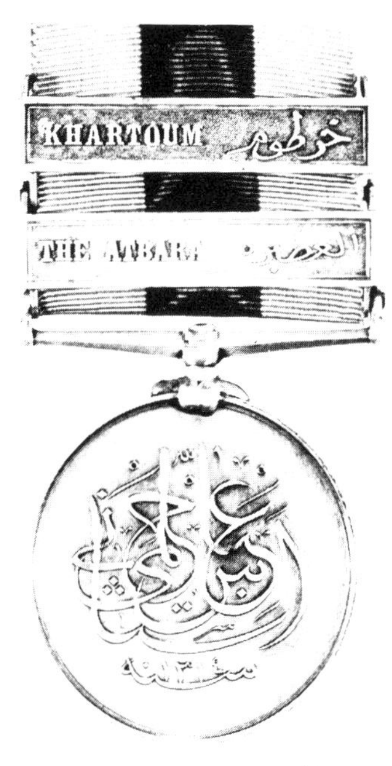

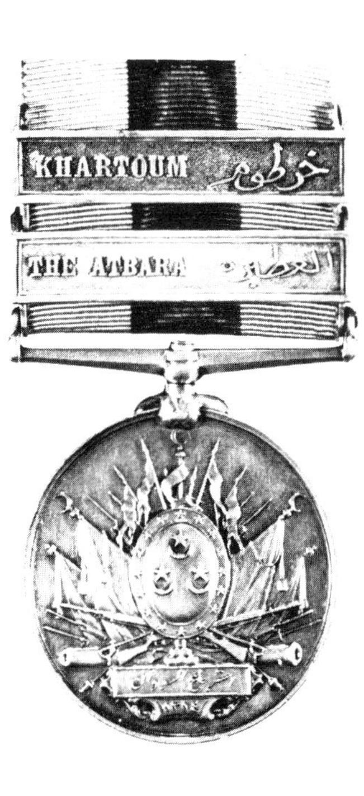

35. Queens' Sudan Medal 1896–97

In 1899 this medal was awarded to the armed forces engaged in the reconquest of the Sudan. The obverse is similar to the East and Central Africa medal (plate 37). The reverse, which is particularly well balanced, shows the seated figure of Victory holding a palm branch in her right hand and a laurel wreath in her left, against a background of four British and Egyptian flags. Her feet rest on a plinth bearing the word SUDAN which is supported by three lilies. The ribbon is yellow and black, divided by a thin vertical stripe of red. These colours are supposed to represent the yellow desert and black dervishes and in between the 'thin red line' of British troops. No battle clasps were issued. Naming varies considerably.

---

36. Khedive's Sudan Medal 1896–1908

Troops engaged in this campaign were also given the Khedive's Sudan Medal which was instituted in 1897 and continued to be awarded until 1908, by which time a total of fifteen bars had been added. It is, however, rarely found with more than two bars (Khartoum and Atbara) to British troops although some Egyptians and Sudanese earned as many as ten clasps. The obverse of the medal carries an Arabic inscription while the reverse shows an oval shield with three stars and crescents thereon, superimposed on a trophy of arms. The whole rests on a plinth inscribed in Arabic THE RE-CONQUEST OF THE SUDAN 1314 (The Mohammedan year 1314 corresponded with 1897 in the Western calendar). The straight suspender holds the 1.5in wide yellow ribbon with a vertical broad blue stripe down the middle, symbolical of the Nile flowing through the desert.

THE ATBARA was awarded for the battle of that name fought on 8th April 1898 against a Dervish army commanded by Emir Mahmoud. It is usually found in conjunction with KHARTOUM which was in fact awarded for the Battle of Omdurman and the famous charge of the 21st Lancers on 2nd September 1898. Although Khartoum was entered after the battle, it is difficult to surmise why a battle clasp should bear any name other than that of the engagement for which it was awarded. No doubt those responsible found ample precedent in that the first two clasps for the 1854 India General Service medal were given for actions outside India (i.e. Burma and Persia) whilst the bar COOMASSIE on the 1873 Ashantee medal commemorates a battle at Amoaful.

The other clasps are as follows:

FIRKET 7th June 1896; HAFIR 19th-26th September 1896; ABU HAMED 7th July 1897; SUDAN 1897 15th July-6th November 1897; GEDAREF 7th September-26th December 1898; GEDID 22nd November 1899; SUDAN 1899; BAHR-EL-GHAZAL 1900-02 13th December 1900-27th April 1902; JEROK January-March 1904; NYAM-NYAM January-May 1905; TALODI 2nd-15th June 1905; KATFIA April 1908; NYIMA 1st-21st November 1908.

37. East and Central Africa 1897–1899

This award superseded the Central Africa Medal 1891-8. On the obverse is the half-length figure of Queen Victoria wearing a small crown and veil and holding a sceptre in her right hand with the familiar legend VICTORIA REGINA ET IMPERATRIX. The obverse shows Britannia holding a trident in her right hand and standing in front of a magnificent British Lion. The sun rises in the right background and in the exergue are the words EAST & CENTRAL AFRICA. The ribbon is half yellow and half red. Naming is in thin sloping or upright capitals. The medal, without bars, was awarded to certain native bearers.

The following four bars were authorised:

LUBWA'S 23rd September 1897-24th February 1898. For operations against a battalion of mutinous Sudanese troops who had to be driven out of Fort Lubwa.

UGANDA 1897-98 20th July 1897-19th March 1898. Military operations in the Protectorate.

1898 21st March-2nd May 1899. Action against a Somali tribe.

UGANDA 1899 21st March-2nd May 1899. Further operations within the Protectorate.

38. Queen's South Africa Medal 11th October 1899–31st May 1902

In common with many other wars which 'will be over by Christmas' it appears that the probable duration of a campaign against some rebellious farmers was grossly underestimated, and the first issue of this medal bore the dates 1899-1900 on the reverse. This was speedily rectified but the dates are still visible on many pieces, especially when they are 'toned'.

'He who fights and runs away lives to fight another day' should have been coined about the Boer, even if it wasn't. Hardy, practical and an expert shot, afraid of nothing other than a cavalry lance (which he regarded as a barbaric weapon to use against white men) the Boer saw nothing glorious in war and had no intention of dying, other than from ripe old age. Having picked off two or three of the 'red-necks' who advanced against him in Aldershot parade ground formation, there was no future in remaining to be bayoneted, nor was there any ignominy in retreat. He would mount his pony, laagered never far to the rear, and gallop off the to the next line of defences to repeat the process, or work round the flanks. Backed by well trained artillery and foreign volunteers, the Boers taught the British soldier lessons in tactics, fieldcraft and sniping. Fourteen years later, these lessons learned and assimilated would enable a British Corps to hold back a German Army at Mons, but in 1899 the lessons had still be learned the hard way at a cost of nearly 30,000 casualties.

The obverse of the medal is similar to plate 42 for the Third China War. The reverse shows Britannia with a standard in her left hand holding out a laurel wreath to advancing troops. In the left background are two men-of-war and following the top half circle are the words SOUTH AFRICA. There were two different strikings of this reverse; in the first Britannia's wreath points to the R in Africa whereas in the second it points to the F. These strikings do not affect the price of the medal. A broad orange band constitutes the middle of the ribbon, which is flanked on either side by a blue stripe and a wider red stripe. Naming varies considerably and owing to the staggering number of Imperial, Colonial, volunteer and auxiliary formations engaged, it is often difficult to decipher a unit which is only represented by initials. C.C.C.C. for example stands for Cape Colony Cyclist Corps and C.M.S.C.-Corps of Military Staff Clerks! Bronze medals without bars were awarded to certain Indian and West Indian troops and native bearers.

Twenty-six bars were issued, of which five are termed 'State' bars, that is they were awarded for various small actions in the various states, two are dated bars and the remainder are battle or engagement clasps. The maximum number of bars to any one medal is nine to the Army and eight to the Navy. Nobody could be awarded both the CAPE COLONY and NATAL bars together, although the medal rolls show that Pte. Wingell, a Royal Marine attached to the army, managed the impossible. The bars are:

CAPE COLONY 11th October 1899-31st May 1902; NATAL 11th October 1899-17th May 1900; RHODESIA 11th October 1899-17th May 1900; RELIEF OF MAFEKING 17th May 1900; DEFENCE OF KIMBERLEY 15th October 1899-15th February 1900; TALANA 20th October 1899; ELANDSLAAGTE 21st October 1899; DEFENCE OF LADYSMITH 3rd November 1899-28th February 1900; BELMONT 23rd November 1899; MODDER RIVER 28th November 1899; TUGELA HEIGHTS 12th-27th February 1900; RELIEF OF KIMBERLEY 15th February 1900; PAADERBERG 17th-26th February 1900; ORANGE FREE STATE 28th February 1900-31st May 1902; RELIEF OF LADYSMITH 15th December 1899-28th February 1900; DRIEFONTEIN 10th March 1900; WEPENER 9th-25th April 1900; DEFENCE OF MAFEKING 13th October 1899–17th May 1900; TRANSVAAL 24th May 1900–31st May 1902; JOHANNESBURG 31st May 1900; LAING'S NEK 12th June 1901; DIAMOND HILL 11th-12th June 1900; WITTEBERGEN 1st-29th July 1900; BELFAST 26th-27th August 1900; SOUTH AFRICA 1901; SOUTH AFRICA 1902.

These last two bars were awarded to those not eligible for the King's medal although they served at the front during 1901 or from 1st January to 31st May 1902.

39. King's South Africa Medal 1901–1902

As Queen Victoria died during the South Africa War, King Edward VII authorised this medal to be awarded to all those who were serving in South Africa on or after 1st January 1902 and would complete eighteen months service before 1st June 1902. It was always issued in conjunction with the Queen's medal and never issued without a bar, except to nearly 600 nursing sisters.

The obverse of the medal is similar to that on the second striking of the 1895 India General Service medal, while the reverse and mounting are the same as the Queen's South Africa medal. The ribbon, however, is green, white and yellow in equal widths.

40. Queen's Mediterranean Medal 1899–1902

This medal is precisely the same as the Queen's South Africa medal, except that the word MEDITERRANEAN is substituted for SOUTH AFRICA on the reverse. It was awarded to garrisons in the Mediterranean, including St. Helena, an important Boer P.O.W. camp. No bars were awarded.

41. Transport Medal 1899 –1902

The obverse has the bust of King Edward VII in the uniform of an Admiral of the Fleet and the legend EDWARDVS VII REX ET IMPERATOR and the reverse shows a map of most of the world with a steamship and below the inscription OB PATRIAM MILITIBUS PER MARE TRANSVECTIS ADJUTAM. The ribbon is red with a blue stripe, 5mm wide inset 3mm from each edge. There are two bars: SOUTH AFRICA 1899-1902 and CHINA 1900. This medal was sanctioned on 8th November 1903 for award to senior officers of troop transports to the South Africa War and the Boxer Rebellion.

(Both this and the preceding award are included only for reference; neither, by any stretch of the imagination, can be termed campaign medals, as it was not possible for the recipient to be in action! Perhaps they are better described as interesting curios.)

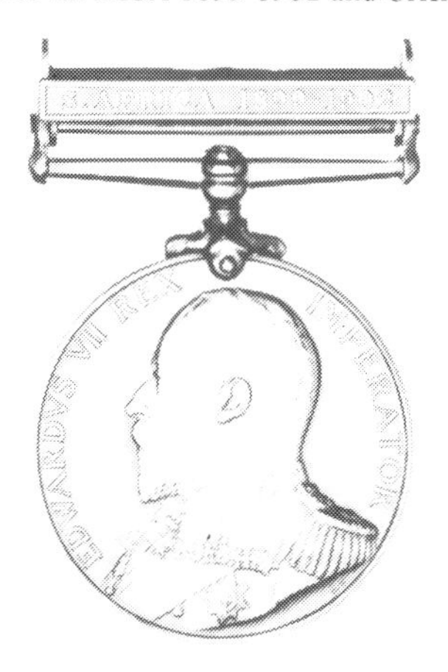

42. Third China War 1900 10th June–31st December 1900

This war is usually known as the Boxer Rebellion, derived from the members of a Chinese secret society known as 'Fists of Righteous Harmony' or 'Boxers'. A wave of looting and murder, including at least one missionary burned alive, proved neither righteous nor harmonious and the major powers landed an allied expeditionary force to restore order.

Although the medal was not issued until the reign of Edward VII, it had been approved by Queen Victoria and bore on the obverse her crowned and veiled head with the legend VICTORIA REGINA ET IMPERATRIX. The reverse was similar to the China medal of 1860 but the date 1900 was added under CHINA in the exergue. The ribbon is crimson with full yellow edges 6mm wide. The naming is indented in thin block capitals. The locally recruited coolie corps received unnamed bronze medals.

The three bars were issued as follows: TAKU FORTS, DEFENCE OF LEGATIONS and RELIEF OF PEKIN. The clasps for the legations were issued to 82 British troops, who formed part of the Legation guard of just over 400, and these are very rare.

43. Ashanti 31st March–25th December 1900

This medal was sanctioned in October 1901 and granted to men of the Ashanti Field Force who had suppressed a native rising. It was the first medal to be awarded in the reign of Edward VII, and the obverse shows his bust with the legend EDWARDVS VII REX IMPERATOR. The reverse portrays a British Lion standing on a rock with a native shield and two assegais thereon. Beneath, in a small scroll, is the word ASHANTI. The sun rises in the left background. The ribbon is dark green with a black stripe 4½mm wide, on each edge and in the centre. One bar inscribed KUMASSI was awarded to troops who defended, or relieved, the town of that name between 31st March and 15th July 1900. The medal in bronze was given to native bearers.

44. Africa General Service Medal 1902–1956

The obverse of this medal is the same as that of the King's South Africa Medal (plate 39) and the reverse is similar to that for East and Central Africa (plate 37), except that the one word AFRICA appears in the exergue. The ribbon is yellow, edged with black and with two narrow green stripes equidistant in the middle.

Thirty-four bars were issued with this medal; a further ten for the second issue bearing the head of King George V and one for the third issue with the head of Queen Elizabeth II. As we have given away, withdrawn from, or been thrown out of our African possessions it seems unlikely that there will ever be a forty-sixth bar to this medal. It would take far too long even to outline the circumstances leading to the award of all these bars; but the list of names on the clasps is as follows:

N.NIGERIA: N.NIGERIA 1902; N.NIGERIA 1903; N.NIGERIA 1903-4; N.NIGERIA 1904; N.NIGERIA 1906; S.NIGERIA; S.NIGERIA 1902; S.NIGERIA 1902-03; S.NIGERIA 1903; S.NIGERIA 1903-04; S.NIGERIA 1904; S.NIGERIA 1904-5; S.NIGERIA 1905; S.NIGERIA 1905-6; UGANDA 1900; EAST AFRICA 1902; EAST AFRICA 1904; EAST AFRICA 1905; EAST AFRICA 1906; WEST AFRICA 1906; WEST AFRICA 1908, WEST AFRICA 1909-10; SOMALILAND 1901; SOMALILAND 1902-4; JIDBALLI; SOMALILAND 1908-10; B.C.A. 1899-1900 (British Central Africa); JUBULAND; GAMBIA; ARO 1901-02; LANGO 1901; KISSI 1905; NANDI 1905-06; SHIMBER BERRIS 1914-15; NYASALAND 1915; EAST AFRICA 1913; EAST AFRICA 1914; EAST AFRICA 1913-14; EAST AFRICA 1915; JUBULAND 1917-18; EAST AFRICA 1918; NIGERIA 1918; SOMALILAND 1920 (the first time troops were conveyed by aircraft carrier, H.M.S. Ark Royal) and KENYA 21st October 1952 to 17th November 1956.

---

45. Tibet Medal 13th December 1903–23rd September 1904

This award was authorised in February 1905 for all members of the Tibet Mission and accompanying troops who served at or beyond Silgari between the dates shown. Very few British troops were present and consquently medals to Europeans are scarce. The obverse carries a bust of Edward VII in Field Marshal's uniform and the legend EDWARDVS VII KAISAR-I-HIND. In shallow relief on the reverse is a representation of the fortress of Lhasa and underneath are the words TIBET 1903-4. The ribbon has a maroon centre flanked by a white stripe on each side and 6mm wide green stripes on each edge. One bar GYANTSE was given to those who defended, or relieved, that fort.

46. Zulu Rebellion 8th February–3rd August 1906

Granted by the Natal Government in 1908 to all those who had taken part in the suppression of the Zulu rising in 1906. On the obverse is the coinage head of King Edward VII and the legend EDWARDVS VII REX IMPERATOR. The reverse is somewhat complicated and has a female figure, representing Natal, holding the sword of Justice in her right hand and a palm branch in her left. She stands on some scattered native weapons and is supported by Britannia. In the background are some natives and a krall, whilst the rising sun shows in the right. The word NATAL appears in the exergue, and the ribbon is crimson with black edges. It was generally issued with a bar with the date 1906 thereon.

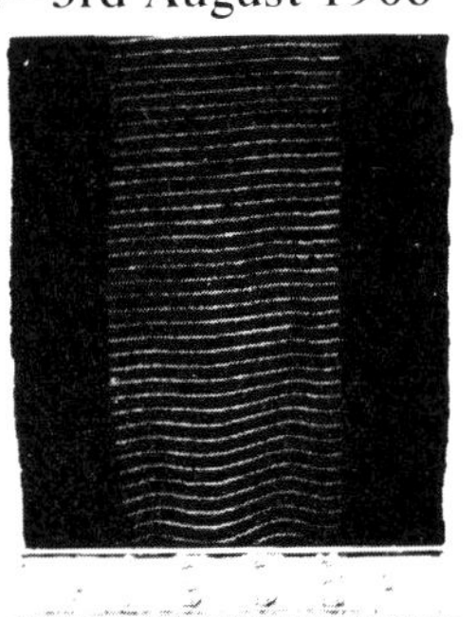

47. India General Service Medal 1908–1935

In December 1908 a new Indian General Service medal was issued for the North West Frontier campaign of that year. It was also the last medal struck in the reign of Edward VII. There were three issues of this particular medal, but the reverse was the same in each case and shows Jamrud Fort with Khyber Pass in the background. Below is the word INDIA partly framed by a branch of laurel and another of oak. The ribbon is green with a dark blue stripe 15mm wide in the centre, and hangs from a floral suspender with rosettes, in common with all previous Indian General Service medals. The obverse of the first issue is similar to the Tibet medal. The second issue, which started with the medal given with the bar for ABOR 1911-12, has the crowned bust of King George V in robes and the legend GEORGIVS V KAISAR-I-HIND. The third issue began with the award given with the bar for NORTH WEST FRONTIER 1930-31 and again showed the crowned bust of King George V in robes, but with the legend GEORGIVS. V.D.G. BRITT. OMN. REX. ET. INDIAE IMP. The medal was issued in both silver and bronze and there were twelve bars issued:

NORTH WEST FRONTIER 1908. This was awarded to the Mohmand Field Force, Bazaar Valley Field Force and for service at Landi Kotal and north of Adinazai.

ABOR 1911-12 6th October 1911-20th April 1912. For an expedition against the Abors and the first bar awarded with the second issue medal.

AFGHANISTAN N.W.F. 1919. This bar was awarded for service in a full-scale campaign which was literally the third Afghan War. After the awards for the first and second Afghan campaigns it seems strange that the third conflict should be dismissed with a clasp - possibly after World War I it would have been incongruous to strike another medal for a minor war.

WAZIRISTAN 1919-21. The Wazirs hastening for their share of plunder and fighting with the invading Afghans and keeping the pot boiling long after their allies had fled back across the frontier.

MAHSUD 1919-20. The aftermath of the third Afghan war.

MALABAR 1921-22. This was awarded for the suppression of the Moplah Rebellion.

WAZIRISTAN 1921-24. A full-scale campaign against the northern and southern Wazirs.

WAZIRISTAN 1925. This was issued to small numbers of R.A.F. personnel and the only bar ever awarded to the R.A.F. exclusive of the other fighting services.

NORTH WEST FRONTIER 1930-31. For operations along the Mohmand border and the first medal of the third issue.

BURMA 1930-32. A series of small actions in Burma lasting fifteen months.

MOHMAND 1933. No British regiments served in this operation.

NORTH WEST FRONTIER 1935. More trouble with the Mohmands.

48. Sudan Medal 1910

Authorised by the Khedive in 1911 to replace the 1897 issue. There was a further issue in 1918 which bore a new date and the cipher of the new Khedive. On the obverse is an Arabic inscription reading ABBAS HILMI THE SECOND and the Mohammedan year 1328. The reverse shows a very fine lion standing with his front paws on a plinth, inscribed SUDAN and in front of the plinth is a trophy of native arms. The background shows the Nile, palm trees and the rising sun. The ribbon, 1.3in wide, has a black watered centre flanked on each side by a thin green stripe and a 5mm wide red stripe.

It was issued unnamed and has sixteen bars, each inscribed in English on the left and Arabic on the right. The bars in chronological order are:

ATWOT February-April 1910; S. KORDOFAN 1910 10th November-19th December 1910; SUDAN 1912 March 1912; ZERAF 1913-14 December 1913-June 1914; MANDAL March 1914; MIRI April 1915; MONGALLA 1915-16 December 1915-March 1916; DARFUR 1916 March-23rd May 1916; FASHER 1st September-23rd November 1916; LAU NUER March-May 1917; NYIMA 1917-18 2nd November 1917-February 1918; ATWOT 1st January-26th May 1918; GARJAK NUER December 1919-April 1920; ALIAB DINKA 8th November 1919-May 1920; NYALA 26th September 1921-20th January 1922; DARFUR 26th September-22nd November 1921.

49. 1914 Star

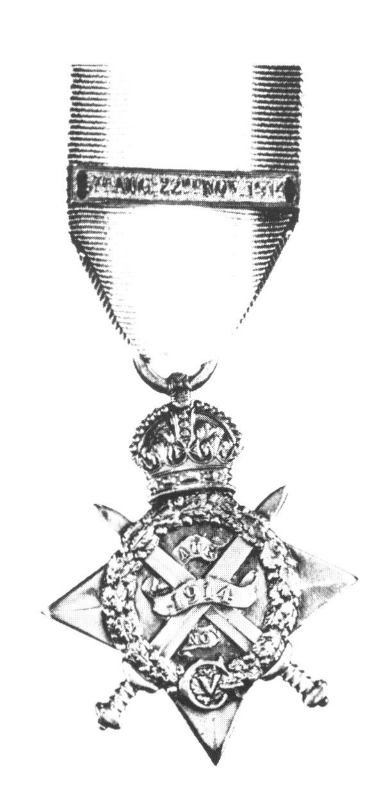

A bronze star with three points, the topmost is replaced by a crown to which is affixed a half-inch diameter ring for suspension; the entire piece is a solid stamping. Across the face of the star are two crossed swords with the points and hilts protruding. In the centre, where the swords cross, is a scroll with the date 1914 thereon and on two small scrolls, one above and one below, are the months AUG and NOV respectively. The scrolls are surrounded by a wide laurel wreath. The reverse is plain and the recipient's number, rank, name and unit are stamped thereon in block capitals.

This star was authorised in April 1917 to be awarded to all those who served in France or Belgium between 5th August and midnight on 22nd/23rd November 1914. Service afloat, in any theatre of war, did not count. In October 1919 a bar was sanctioned to all those who had been under fire in either country between the qualifying dates for the star. This bar is bronze with the inscription 5TH AUG-22ND NOV. 1914 on a frosted ground. Unlike previous clasps it has a small hole in each corner to enable it to be sewn directly on to the ribbon. Those entitled to the bar wear a small silver rosette when only ribbons are worn. The ribbon is red, white and blue, shaded and watered.

---

50. 1914–1915 Star 5th August 1914–31st December 1915

This star and ribbon, sanctioned in 1918, is identical to the 1914 Star, except that the two smaller scrolls are omitted and the centre scroll bears the dates 1914-15. It was awarded to all who saw service in any theatre of war, including the North West Frontier in 1915, but not to those who only saw service for which the Africa General Service or the Sudan 1910 medal was granted. Recipients of the 1914 Star were not eligible for the 1914-15 Star. The insignia GV appears at the bottom of the wreath.

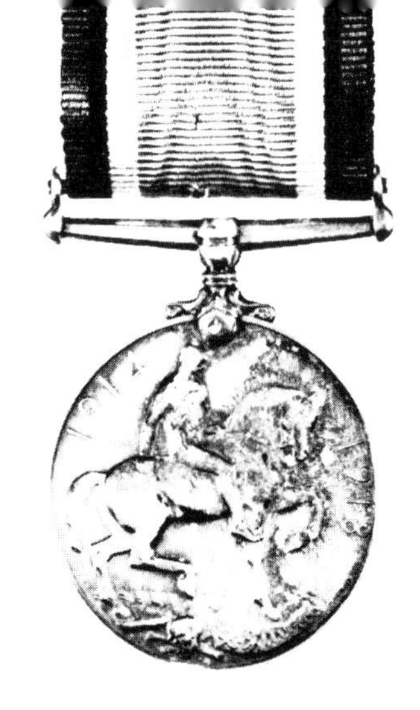

51. British War Medal 1914–1920

This simple silver medal, once commonly seen in pawnbrokers and jewellers windows, commemorates some of the bloodiest battles, fought under the most ghastly conditions, the world has ever known. Although the award is dated 1914-1918 it was in fact issued for certain operations up to 1920, chiefly postwar mine clearance and service in various parts of Russia.

The obverse has the coinage head of King George V with the legend GEORGIVS V BRITT : OMN : REX ET IND : IMP. On the reverse is St. George on horseback trampling the shield of the Central Powers. Underneath is a skull and crossbones, the symbol of death, and above is the risen sun of victory. Around the upper edge are the dates 1914 and 1918. The suspender does not swivel and the ribbon has a broad orange watered centre flanked on each side by white, black and blue stripes. Over five and a half million of these medals were issued, and just over 100,000 bronze medals were awarded to native Labour Corps. It was issued singly without the Victory medal to certain personnel who did not actually serve in a theatre of war.

No bars were issued, although the subject of battle clasps was considered in 1919 by both a Naval and Military committee. The idea was finally shelved on the ground of cost, but it is interesting that the final Admiralty proposals were approved by H.M. The King and printed in an Admiralty Order in 1920. This gave a substantial list of actions and operations, totalling 49 in all. (My father had worked out that he would have been entitled to seven, including JUTLAND and was most annoyed at the stinginess of the Government.)

52. Mercantile Marine War Medal 1914–1918

This medal was issued, but only in bronze, by the Board of Trade to members of the Merchant Navy who served at least one voyage in a danger zone, or six months at sea in certain named occupations, (i.e. pilot ships and lighthouse vessels). The obverse is similar to the British War Medal. The reverse shows the bows of a merchant steamer ploughing through a heavy sea with a sailing vessel in the background and a sinking U-boat in the right foreground. In the exergue in three lines appears FOR WAR SERVICE MERCANTILE MARINE 1914-1918. The ribbon is watered green and red with a thin white stripe down the centre and the colours are supposed to indicate the port, starboard and steaming lights of a ship. Only the recipient's name appears on the edge in indented block capitals.

53. Victory Medal 1914–1918

This bronze medal was awarded to all who were awarded either of the Stars and, with few exceptions, to recipients of the British War Medal. Men who were mentioned in despatches were allowed to wear a bronze oak leaf on the ribbon. The obverse of the medal shows the winged, standing figure of Victory with a palm branch in her right hand and the reverse carries the inscription THE GREAT WAR FOR CIVILIZATION 1914-1919 surrounded by a wreath. The ribbon is 1.55in wide with a rainbow pattern with the colours merging; from the centre, outwards to each edge, they are red, yellow, green, blue and violet. The ribbon is threaded through a half-inch diameter ring which is held by a small loop sweated to the top of the medal. Naming is in faint, impressed capitals giving the recipient's number, rank, name and unit. But in the case of officers only the rank and name is given.

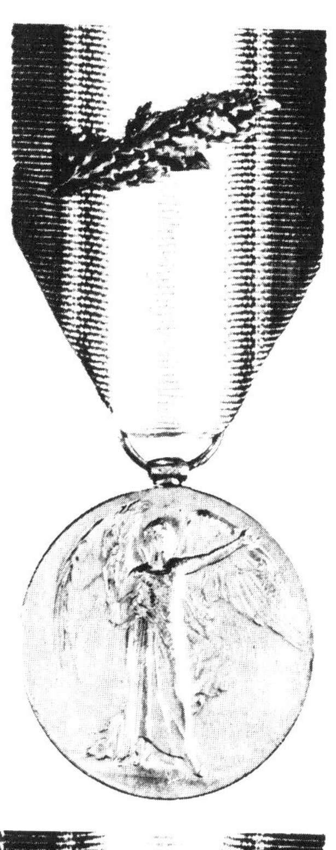

54. Territorial Force War Medal 1914–1919

This bronze medal was authorised in April 1920 for members of the Territorial Force including nursing sisters who, on or before 30th September 1914, undertook to serve outside the United Kingdom, did so between the outbreak of war and the armistice, and were not eligible for either the 1914 or 1914-15 Star.

The obverse is similar to the British War Medal. On the reverse, following the upper half circle of the piece, are the words TERRITORIAL WAR MEDAL, whilst in the centre, within a laurel wreath, is the inscription FOR VOLUNTARY SERVICE OVERSEAS 1914-19. This is yet another instance where the date shown on a medal has nothing in common with the qualifying date for the award. The ribbon is watered yellow with a green vertical stripe, 4½mm wide, a similar distance from each edge. Naming is in impressed block capitals showing the number, rank, name and unit.

55. Naval General Service Medal 1915–1964

Although the first bar to this medal is dated 1909, the award itself for minor naval operations was not instituted until 1915. There have been strikings. The first issue, spanning the first three bars, has on the obverse the head of King George V wearing the uniform of Admiral of the Fleet with the legend GEORGIVS V BRITT: OMN: REX ET IND : IMP. The second issue, covering the period 1936 to 1952 has the crowned coinage head of King George VI and the legend GEORGIVS VI : BR : OMN : REX ET INDIAE IMP. The third bears the crowned bust of Queen Elizabeth II with the legend ELIZABETH II D : G : BR: OMN : REGINA F : D. A fourth carries the legend ELIZABETH II DEI GRATIA REGINA: F : D:. The reverse is the same in every issue and shows Britannia on two sea-horses, her left hand resting on a Union Shield, riding through the waves. The ribbon is white with crimson edges 4½mm wide and a narrow crimson stripe spaced 5½mm away from the inside edge of the outer colour.

Fifteen bars were awarded as follows:

PERSIAN GULF 1909-1914. Awarded for operations against gun runners, pirates and slavers in the Persian Gulf Area.

IRAQ 1919-20. For service in river gunboats on the Euphrates and Tigris during the Arab Rebellion.

N.W. PERSIA 1920. Issued to two officers and two ratings who served in the Naval Mission.

PALESTINE 1936-1939. Awarded in connection with the 'troubles'.

S.E. ASIA 1945-46. Operations in the Java, Sumatra areas and French Indo-China.

MINESWEEPING 1945-51. Awarded for six months' minesweeping in specified waters.

PALESTINE 1945-48. Renewal of the 'troubles'.

MALAYA 16th June to 14th July 1948.

YANGTZE 1949. Awarded to personnel of all three services connected with the attack on H.M.S. Amethyst and three other vessels by Chinese Communist forces.

BOMB AND MINE CLEARANCE 1945-53. Operations as stated in specified area.

BOMB AND MINE CLEARANCE, MEDITERRANEAN. Self-explanatory.

CYPRUS. Eoka operations 1955-1959.

NEAR EAST. Commemorates the operations on the Suez Canal 1956.

ARABIAN PENINSULAR. 1957-1960.

BRUNEI. Brunei, North Borneo and Sarawak. December 1962.

56. The General Service Medal 1918–1964 (Army and Royal Air Force)

This medal was instituted in 1923 for award with appropriate bars for minor campaigns which did not justify a separate medal (similar to the warrant for the preceding Naval General Service medal).

There are six issues of this medal, each with a different obverse. The obverse and clasps for each issue are as follows: 1. Coinage head of King George V with the legend GEORGIVS V BRITT: OMN: REX ET IND: IMP. S. Persia, Kurdistan, Iraq, N.W. Persia and Southern Desert: Iraq. 2. Crowned head of King George V and legend GEORGIVS V D.G. BRITT. OMN. REX. ET. INDIAE IMP. Northern Kurdistan. 3. Crowned head of King George VI. Legend reads GEORGIVS VI: D: G: BR: OMN: REX ET INDIAE IMP:. Palestine, S.E. Asia 1945-46, Bomb and Mine Clearance 1945-49 and Palestine 1945-48. 4. As 3, but revised legend - GEORGIVS VI DEI GRA: BRITT: OMN: REX FID: DEF: + Palestine 1945-48 and Malaya. 5. Crowned head of Queen Elizabeth II and legend ELIZABETH II D: G: BR: OMN: REGINA F: D:. Malaya. 6. As 5, but legend reads ELIZABETH II DEI GRATIA REGINA F.D. Malaya, Cyprus, Near East, Arabian Peninsular and Brunei.

The reverse is similar for each striking and shows the standing figure of Victory holding a laurel wreath over the emblems of the two Services.

The fifteen bars awarded are as follows:

S. PERSIA. Operations near Bushire and Banda Abbas in 1918 and 1919.

KURDISTAN. For peace keeping and skirmishes in 1919 and 1923. The late date is significant as it was the first time troops were air lifted.

IRAQ. An Arab rebellion in Iraq in 1919 and 1920.

N.W. PERSIA. For the North Persia Force in 1920.

SOUTHERN DESERT, IRAQ. For services in the Southern Desert in 1928 and awarded solely to R.A.F. units.

NORTHERN KURDISTAN. For operations in 1932.

PALESTINE. For the troubles in 1936-1939.

S.E. ASIA 1945-46. An interesting bar covering post-war operations in Java, Sumatra and French Indo-China.

Java, Sumatra and French Indo-China.

BOMB AND MINE CLEARANCE 1945-49. Self-explanatory and largely for operations in the U.K.

PALESTINE 1945-48. Back to the troubles.

MALAYA. Anti-communist operations in Colony of Singapore from 1948 to 1950 and the Federation of Malaya for two months in 1960.

CYPRUS. For operations from 1955 to 1959.

NEAR EAST. The Suez Canal landings in 1956.

ARABIAN PENINSULAR. For service in the Gulf States, Sultanates of Muscat and Oman and the Colony and Protectorate of Aden from 1957 to 1960.

BRUNEI. For operations in Brunei, North Borneo and Sarawak in December 1962.

57. India General Service Medal 1936–1939

This medal was instituted in 1938 and replaced the 1908 award. There are two different strikings, one from England and the second minted in Calcutta. The latter is slightly thicker and the general finish is poor compared with the English striking. The obverse of the medal shows the crowned coinage head of King George VI and the legend GEORGIVS VI D : G : BR : OMN : REX ET INDIAE IMP. On the reverse is a rather peculiar shaped tiger apparently trying to bite his tail. Above him is the word INDIA and below is rocky ground. The ribbon has a stone colour centre flanked by a thin red stripe on each side and green edges 6mm wide. An ornamental suspender and rosettes of typical India medal pattern. Naming is in thin impressed capitals. There are two bars: NORTH WEST FRONTIER 1936-37 and NORTH WEST FRONTIER 1937-1939.

58. 1939–1945 Star (3rd September 1939–15th August 1945)

Although the second World War officially ended on 2nd September 1945 active operations against Japan ceased on 15th August 1945. The qualifications for this award were as follows: for the Royal Navy six months service afloat in areas of active operations were required. For the Army six months service in an operational command were required, but only one days service in Dunkirk, Norway and certain specified commando raids. Airborne troops qualified for the star on participating in an airborne operation provided they had completed two months service in an operational unit. The R.A.F. qualified for the award for any flying operations against the enemy, provided that two months service had been completed in operational units; ground crew had to complete six months service in the area of an operational command except for Dunkirk and Norway. For Merchant Navy personnel qualified for six months service afloat with at least one voyage through specified 'dangerous waters'–the latter including service during the evacuation from Dunkirk. Irrespective of the six months qualification period, all service personnel qualified once they were decorated or mentioned in despatches, killed in action or died on service, evacuated as the result of wounds or sickness on service, or were evacuated from Dunkirk, Norway, Crete and Greece. The time spent as a prisoner of war also counted. Air crews of fighter aircraft engaged in the Battle of Britain between 10th July and 31st October 1940 were awarded a bar inscribed BATTLE OF BRITAIN. A silver-gilt rose emblem takes the place of the bar when only a ribbon is worn, and this applied to all other bars issued for World War II.

In common with the remaining campaign stars, the 1939-45 award is a six-pointed bronze star with a ring, embodied at the head of the top point, which holds the suspension ring. In the centre is the Royal Cypher surmounted by a crown. The latter is superimposed on a circlet which bears the title of the star. The reverse is plain and unnamed (a penny pinching decision which reduced the value of the award to both the recipient and subsequent collectors). The ribbon has three equal stripes of dark blue, red and light blue, representing the services.

59. The Atlantic Star 3rd September 1939–8th May 1945

This award was granted for six months service afloat in the Atlantic, Home Waters, convoys to Russia or certain parts of the South Atlantic. Personnel of the Royal Navy qualified provided they had first earned the 1939-1945 Star for six months service in an operational area and, with minor differences, the same held for men of the Merchant Navy. Air crews qualified for any operation against the enemy in the specified areas, provided they had two months service in an operational unit, and the prior award of the 1939-45 Star. Army and R.A.F. personnel serving with the Royal or Merchant Navy qualified in the same way as members of the service to which they were attached. Those who were not able to complete the qualifying period and were not eligible for the 1939-45 Star were awarded the Atlantic Star. In common with the other campaign stars, any length of service terminated by death or disability, or where the recipient was decorated or mentioned in despatches, also qualified. Two bars were issued, AIR CREW EUROPE and FRANCE AND GERMANY, but not more than one could be earned by any one man. The ribbon is shaded and watered blue, white and sea green.

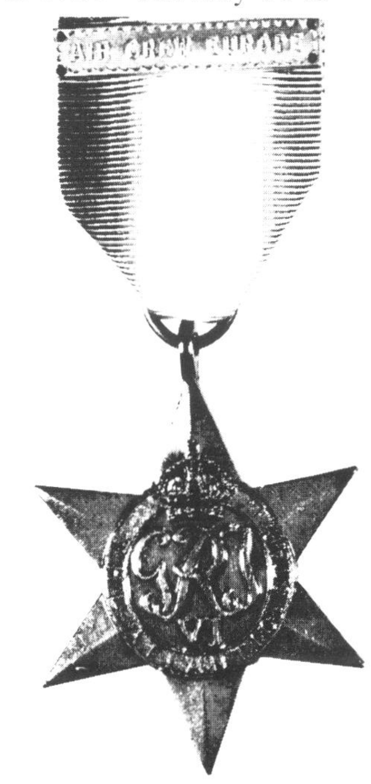

---

60. The Air Crew Europe Star 3rd September 1939–5th June 1944

This star, the rarest of the World War II stars was awarded for operational flying from United Kingdom bases over Europe (including the United Kingdom) for two months. Service in operations at sea did not count. Two bars were issued ATLANTIC or FRANCE AND GERMANY. The ribbon is pale blue flanked by a narrow black stripe on each side and black edges, symbolizing the continuous day and night flying of the R.A.F. This is also one of the stars which have been copied. There are a number of differences, but the most striking is the fact that in the Royal Cypher, the top of the V and I are joined in the original, but separated in the copy.

61. The Africa Star 10th June 1940–12th May 1942

The qualification for this Star was one or more days service in (or in the case of the R.A.F. over) North Africa between 10th June 1940 and 12th May 1943, or Abyssina, Italian Somaliland, Sudan, Eritrea and Malta. Royal or Merchant Navy service anywhere at sea in the Mediterranean also qualified.

Three bars were awarded which consisted of: 1. 8TH ARMY for service in the Eighth Army between 23rd October 1942 and 12th May 1943. 2. 1ST ARMY for service in the First Army, or any unit under the command of that army from 31st December 1942 to 12th May 1943 and 3. NORTH AFRICA 1942-43 to Naval, R.A.F. and Merchant Navy personnel operating in specified areas from 23rd October 1942 to 12th May 1943. When only ribbons are worn these clasps are replaced by 1, the arabic numeral '8'; 2, the arabic numeral '1'; and 3, a small silver rosette. During the same dates inshore service by the Merchant Navy, certain commands of the R.A.F. and the personnel of the Headquarters of 18th Army Group earned a silver rose emblem instead of one of the bars. Although an individual might qualify for all three clasps he was only awarded the one to which he was first entitled.

The ribbon is pale buff with a wide red stripe in the centre. Equidistant between the edges of the ribbon and the middle stripe are a thin dark blue stripe on the left and a thin pale blue stripe on the right. The colours represent the services and the sand of the desert.

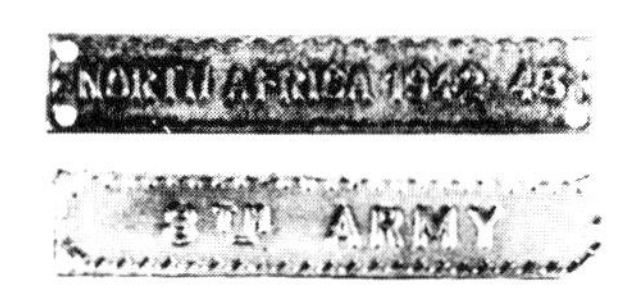

62. The Pacific Star 8th Decembe

Naval and R.A.F. crews had to complete at least one operational sortie over certain specified land or sea areas before being eligible for this award. In the case of the Army there was no prior time qualification but only service in the Pacific theatre of operations in territories invaded by Allied or enemy forces. Hence those unfortunates who disembarked at Singapore and were marched straight into Japanese prisoner-of-war camps earned a Pacific Star (and earned it in a very hard way) despite the fact they were never in action.

This is a multi-coloured ribbon with a pale yellow stripe down the middle, flanked by a green stripe on each side, a narrow dark blue stripe on the right, a pale blue narrow stripe on the left and wider red edges. The colours are symbolical of the jungles and beaches of the Pacific and fighting services. There is one bar BURMA.

63. The Burma Star 11th December 1941–2nd September 1945

The Army qualified for this award for operational service in Burma during the whole of the period, in Bengal and Assam between 1st May 1942 and 2nd September 1945. Service in China and Malaya between 16th February 1942 and the last date was also included. R.A.F. air crew qualified with one operational flight over those areas, but ground crew and staff were subject to similar rules as the Army. Awards to the Royal and Merchant Navies were confined to a large area of the Bay of Bengal, including the Malacca Strait.

The ribbon has a broad red central stripe flanked on either side by a blue stripe of similar width. In the centre of each of the blue edges is a narrow orange stripe. One bar PACIFIC was issued with this Star.

941–2nd September 1945

64. Italy Star 11th June 1943–8th May 1945

Although termed the Italy Star it was awarded for active service in Italy, Sicily, Greece, Yugoslavia, Corsica, Sardinia, Elba and the Aegean and Dodecanese. However, service in Sicily after 17th August 1943, Sardinia after 19th September 1943 and in Corsica after 4th October 1943 did not qualify. Generally speaking, entry into Austrian territory during the closing stages of the war also qualified. R.A.F. air crew who took part in operations within the Mediterranean theatre, including operations over Europe from Mediterranean bases, also qualified. Conditions for R.A.F. ground forces and Naval shore parties were similar to those for army personnel. The Royal Navy and the merchant service personnel qualified by service afloat in and around the areas mentioned and including operations off the south of France.

The ribbon is five equal widths of red, white, green, white and red, representing the Italian national colours. There were no bars for this award, and thus the Italy Star was also granted in addition to other stars.

65. The France and Germany Star 6th June 1944–8th May 1945

This Star was awarded for operational service in France, Belgium, Holland and Germany between the dates shown, that is from D-Day until the German surrender. Royal and Merchant Navy personnel qualified with service afloat in direct support of land operations. Air crews were eligible for service against the enemy over Europe, except flights which emanated from the Mediterranean area. Naval landing parties and non-aircrew personnel qualified under the same conditions as the Army.

The colours of the ribbon are blue, white, red, white and blue in equal widths and represent the colours of the Union Jack, France and the Netherlands. There was one bar ATLANTIC. In common with the other campaign stars which also carried bars, a recipient was only awarded the star for which he first qualified, plus one bar for further service. There was no AIR CREW EUROPE clasp.

66. The Defence Medal 3rd September 1939–15th August 1945

This cupro-nickel medal has the coinage head of King George VI with the usual legend on the obverse. The reverse shows the Royal Crown resting above a small oak tree and flanked by two heraldic lions. The dates 1939 and 1945 appear in the top left and right respectively, whilst beneath the design are the words THE DEFENCE MEDAL. The ribbon is flame coloured with green edges and symbolises the air attacks and destruction on our green land. The nationwide black-out is represented by a narrow black stripe down the centre of each of the green edges. Generally speaking, this medal was awarded for three years service in Great Britain until 8th May 1945 or six months overseas in territories subjected to, or threatened by enemy attacks. The time was extended to forces overseas until 15th August 1945, the end of the war in the Pacific. In the case of mine and bomb disposal units the time qualification was three months.

Owing to the terms of reference for campaign awards it is not unusual to find a man with several stars who has never heard a shot fired in anger. Conversely, a man with only the Defence Medal who earned it, for example, whilst serving with the fire or rescue services in London or any other city subjected to constant air attack, wears a medal worth having. In common with all other decorations and medals only the man who wears the medal knows how it was earned.

67. The War Medal 3rd September 1939–2nd September 1945

This medal is also cupro-nickel and on the obverse has the crowned head of King George VI with the usual legend. On the reverse is a British Lion standing over a vanquished dragon. The dates 1939 and 1945 appear in two lines in the top right. The ribbon embodies the colours of the Union Jack and is red, blue, white, blue and red in equal widths. A thin red stripe runs down the centre of the white portion. It was awarded to all full time personnel of the armed forces who completed twenty-eight days service during the qualifying dates. For merchant seamen there was a separate requirement, that the twenty-eight days must have been served at sea. Service terminated by death, wounds or capture also qualified. Thus a man taken prisoner at Dunkirk has two ribbons to show for his five years' captivity, the 1939-45 Star and the War Medal.

The War Medal ribbon may also carry one bronze oak leaf emblem signifying the wearer has been mentioned in despatches, irrespective of the theatre of war or the number of times mentioned.

68. The Korea Medal 2nd July 1950–10th June 1953

There are two issues of this medal which differ only in the legend on the obverse. Both show the laureated head of Queen Elizabeth II, but whereas the first type has the wording ELIZABETH II DEI GRA : BRITT : OMN : REGINA F : D:, the second is worded ELIZABETH II DEI. GRATIA. REGINA F:D. One school of thought believes that the second issue is an error, but this is difficult to believe. It is cupro-nickel, but the medal issued by Canada is silver, and has the word CANADA beneath the Queen's head. On the reverse is Hercules, armed with a short sword fighting the many-headed Hydra. In the exergue is the word KOREA. The ribbon has five equal stripes of yellow, blue, yellow, blue and yellow. The naming is impressed in thin capitals.

The medal was sanctioned in 1951 for award to members of the British Commonwealth Forces who fought on behalf of the United Nations on the side of South Korea. One day's service in Korea qualified personnel of any of the three services or twenty-eight days sea service in the operational areas of the Yellow Sea and Sea of Japan for the Royal Navy. R.A.F. personnel qualified either in accordance with the rules for the Navy and Army, or one operational sortie over Korea or Korean waters. Anyone awarded the Korea medal also received the United Nations medal with bar KOREA. This medal is made of bronze alloy and has a very cheap appearance. The ribbon has seventeen alternate vertical stripes of blue and white.

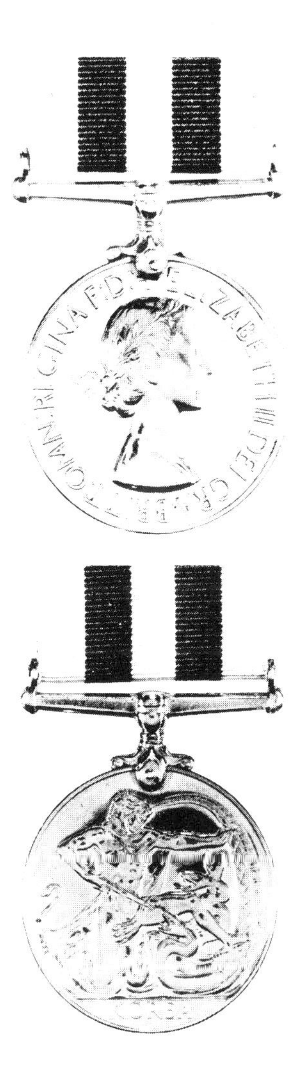

69. The Campaign Service Medal, 1962 to date

As the three armed services were amalgamated under one ministry, the Ministry of Defence, a new medal was instituted in 1964 for award to all the fighting sevices. The obverse (similar to No. 70) carries the crowned effigy of Queen Elizabeth II with the legend ELIZABETH II DEI GRATIA REGINA F:D, and the reverse has the words FOR CAMPAIGN SERVICE surrounded by a laurel wreath. It has an ornamental swivelling suspender, similar to that of the obsolete General Service medal, and the ribbon is purple with green edges. Naming is in impressed small block capitals. The bars awarded so far are:

1 BORNEO. Service against the rebels in North Borneo, Sarawak or Brunei from 24th December 1962 until 11th August 1966.
2 RADFAN. Operations in the South Arabian Federation from 23rd April to 31st July 1964.
3 SOUTH VIETNAM. Awarded only to Australian and New Zealand Forces, 24th December 1962 to 29th May 1964.
4 SOUTH ARABIA. For services in that area from 1st August 1964 to 30th November 1967.
5 MALAY PENINSULA. 17th August 1964 to 11th August 1966.
6 NORTHERN IRELAND. 14th August 1969 onwards.
7 DHOFAR. 1st October 1969 to 30th September 1976.
8 LEBANON. 7th February 1983 to 9th March 1984, peacekeeping force. Thirty days' service, not necessarily continuous, including territorial waters.
9 MINE CLEARANCE – GULF OF SUEZ. Thirty accumulated days of service between 15th August and 15th October 1984. About 300 servicemen qualified for this clasp plus Merchant Navy seamen on board S.S. *Oil Endeavour*.
10. GULF. Minesweeping in the Persian Gulf and the Gulf of Oman between 17th November 1986 and 31st October 1988. Also for subsequent mining countermeasures in the same waters from 1st November 1988 to 28th February 1989. Thirty days' service, not necessarily continuous. British personnel on Dutch and Belgian vessels and Royal Fleet auxiliaries, but not the Sultan of Oman's Navy, were entitled to this clasp.
11. KUWAIT. Thirty continuous days in Kuwait, and its territorial waters, and the Northern Gulf north of 28° 30'N and west of 49° 30'E, between 8th March and 30th September 1991. .
12. N IRAQ & S TURKEY. Thirty days' continuous service, or three operational sorties, in Northern Iraq west of 44° 45E and north of 36° 00'N, and Southern Turkey, including its territorial waters, east of 35° 00'E and south of 38° 00'N, between 6 April and 17 July 1991. Multinational personnel serving with units of Operation HAVEN received this clasp, but not Dutch personnel, who received a comparable award from their own Government.

70. The Australian and New Zealand Vietnam Service Medal 1964–1973

The terms of the Royal Warrant restrict this award to members of the Australian and New Zealand armed forces serving in Vietnam between 29th May 1964 and 27th January 1973. By the same token it was possible for a man to earn both this and the preceding medal in cases where his tour of duty overlapped the qualifying date.

On the obverse of the medal is the crowned effigy of Queen Elizabeth II with the legend ELIZABETH II DEI GRATIA REGINA F.D. The reverse has a symbolical representation of the ideological war in Vietnam and depicts a naked man, left hand outstretched, holding back an encroaching sphere. Behind him is another sphere and following the curve of the medal, above his head, the word VIETNAM.

The ribbon is bordered on the left by a dark blue stripe and on the right by a light blue stripe, each 6mm wide. Both blue margins are flanked by a red stripe 3mm wide. The remainder of the ribbon is yellow apart from three vertical equidistant red stripes, each 1mm wide and the same distance apart, in the middle. The colours represent the three armed services and the national colours of Vietnam.

71. The South Atlantic Medal 2nd April–14th June 1982

Struck in cupro-nickel with the Imperial crowned head of Queen Elizabeth II on the obverse and the legend ELIZABETH II DEI GRATIA REGINA FID. DEF. The reverse bears the arms of the Falkland Islands beneath the words SOUTH ATLANTIC and above a laurel wreath. A fixed suspender supports the ribbon, which has five vertical stripes of equal width, shaded and watered, in empire blue, white, sea green, white and empire blue. The naming is impressed in small capitals on the rim and, when awarded to Royal Navy personnel, includes the ship's name. This is omitted on medals to crews of Royal Fleet auxiliaries and vessels temporarily commissioned from trade. In addition, there are some unusual abbreviations such as N.L.P. 21 (Naval Landing Party No. 21).

The medal was awarded first for service of one day or more in the Falkland Islands or their dependencies, or in the South Atlantic south of 35° South and north of 60° South, or in any operational aircraft sortie. For practical purposes this definition embraces the southern part of the South Atlantic, the Falkland Islands and South Georgia. Within these limits, and in the absence of any curtailing degrees of latitude, it would include any forces landing upon or flying over the mainland of South America. Medals earned in this section carry a rosette on the ribbon; a cheap way of saving the cost of striking three different and hard-won clasps. The second qualification, for medals without a rosette, was service of 30 days or more in the South Atlantic south of 7° South and north of 35° South. This is virtually the northern part of the South Atlantic and includes the Ascension Islands (main supply base for the campaign). About 36,000 medals were issued; the smallest number per arm of service was 2,004 to the R.A.F.

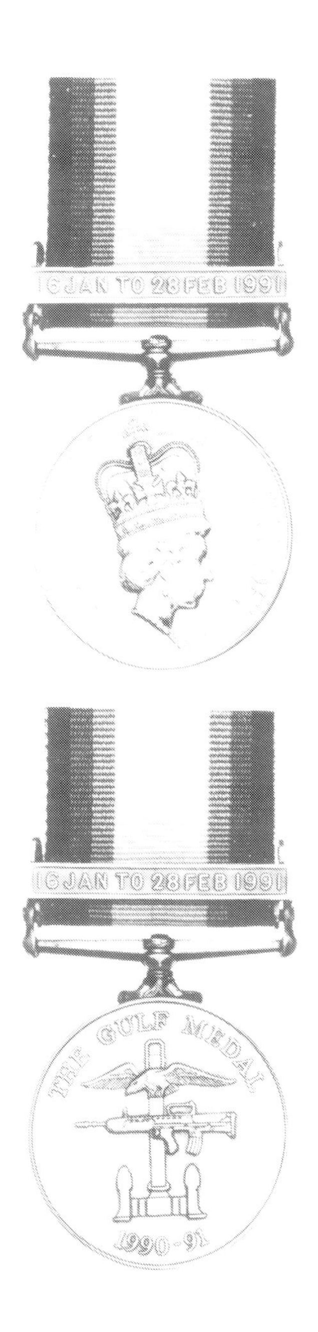

72.The Gulf Medal

A cupro-nickel medal bearing the same obverse as the South Atlantic award (71). On the reverse, a R.A.F. eagle and an SA80 infantry rifle are superimposed upon a modern sea anchor. The dates 1990–91 are shown below the anchor's flukes and THE GULF MEDAL follows the upper curve of the medal. A swivelling suspender holds the ribbon which has a pale buff centre, ½" wide, flanked on each side by ⅛" wide strips of light blue, red and dark blue. These colours denote the desert sand and the three armed Services. There are three different qualifications for this medal, as follows:

(i) Thirty days' continuous service, between 2 August 1990 and 7 March 1991, in Saudi Arabia, Oman, The United Arab Emirates, Qatar, Jordan, Bahrain, Kuwait, Iraq, Republic of Yemen, The Gulf, the Gulf of Oman, the Gulf of Aqaba, the Gulf of Suez and the Suez Canal, the Arabian Sea, the Gulf of Aden and Red Sea, Cyprus and adjacent waters; the Sovereign Base Areas, plus the airspace and high seas of the Eastern Mediterranean. All these areas bounded by curtailing limits of latitude and longitude.

(ii) Service of seven days continuously between 16th January and 28th February 1991 in Saudi Arabia, Bahrain, Kuwait, Iraq, The United Arab Emirates, Oman, Qatar, the Gulf of Oman, the north west Arabian Sea, the Gulf of Aden, The Gulf and the Red Sea. Or, one operational combat sortie (participating directly in the air campaign and including all Nimrod and air-to-air refuelling missions); or, eight sectors in the Arabian Peninsula Flight Information Region by air transport crews.

(iii) Service in the Kuwait Liaison Team in Kuwait on 2nd August 1990.

Medals to those who qualify under (ii) above will carry a clasp with the dates '16 Jan–28 Feb 1991' and for (iii), a bar with the single date '2 Aug 1990'.

Personnel qualifying under the terms of (ii) have also been awarded the Saudi 'Liberation of Kuwait' medal, which H.M. The Queen has directed may be accepted as a keepsake but not worn.